Deck Machinery

J. Rae & Sons Ltd.
Halifax, N.S. B3R 2B4
Telex 019-22773
Catalogue On Request

Also by Percy de W. Smith

Modern Marine Electricity and Electronics

To my wife, Tyyne Marie Lainio Smith

Deck
Machinery

By

PERCY DE WILLARD SMITH

CORNELL MARITIME PRESS, INC.

Cambridge   1973   *Maryland*

Library of Congress Cataloging in Publication Data

Smith, Percy de Willard,   1900–
    Deck machinery.

    1. Deck machinery.   I. Title.
VM781.S57   623.85   73-12704
ISBN   0-87033-185-X

STUDENT TEXT BOOK

No. ENG DEC 1973 c.12

Contents

Publisher's Note: Diagrams included in a separate case accompanying this manual are for the following figure numbers: Figs. 81, 82, 83, 88, 89 and 90.

Preface

The modern cargo ship's deck machinery is a far cry from the old steam winch and coal-burning donkey boiler. Today the very compact fluid motors and electric motors provide the driving power for more efficiently designed winches and windlasses. Since this book is on and about the deck equipment itself, the writer of necessity must lean heavily on the equipment manufacturer for information.

The author is therefore deeply indebted to the many sources who have provided photographs, drawings, circuit diagrams, maintenance information, operating instructions, and other descriptive material and wishes especially to thank the Denison Division of the Abex Corporation, Hyde Products, Inc., Lake Shore, Inc., Reliance Electric Company and the Westinghouse Corporation.

It is hoped that seagoing engineers and the maintenance personnel, as well as shipbuilders, will find this manual useful.

Percy de Willard Smith

Introduction

The cargo ship of today is equipped with a wide range of deck machinery designed for docking, cargo handling and other miscellaneous services.

The docking equipment includes the anchor windlass, capstans, warping winches, constant tension mooring winches and the steering gear.

The cargo handling machinery includes cargo winches, heavy lift winches, boom topping winches, preventer guy winches, gantry cranes for container handling, deck cranes with 360° swing, traveling cranes running both fore and aft and athwartship, and mechanized boom and rigging having preventer guy winches and arranged for joy stick* operation.

Miscellaneous services include lifeboat winches, hatch cover winches, hose handling cranes, accommodation ladder winches, towing machinery, dredge hoists, fishing trawler winches, oceanographic winches with 20,000—30,000 feet or more of acoustical or hydrographic cable.

In recent years great emphasis has been placed on more efficient cargo handling, resulting in shorter turn-around time. This brought into being the container ships and the LASH (Lighter Aboard Ship) ships with their heavier unit loads and 500-ton capacity gantry cranes. Heavy lift cargo gear and cranes are now quite common, requiring the design of new masts. Notable among these are the "Hallen derrick," the Wardill and Stulcken masts.

Fully mechanized hatch covers are standard equipment, the size of which was unheard of a few years ago.

Figure 1 shows cargo handling gear aboard a modern cargo ship. Note the winch control station between the king posts.

---

*Usually a portable control box with levers (joy sticks) which may be moved in several directions, namely for hoisting, for lowering, to right or to left, the latter for swinging the boom through winch driven preventer guys. The joy stick springs back to a vertical neutral position when released.

Fig. 1. Deck view of an American Lines vessel. This is a typical installation of hoisting machinery showing cargo winches, topping winches, vang or preventer guy winches and central winch control station. (Balin - Pl. (i) C.)

CHAPTER I

Anchor Windlass

The anchor windlass will be found in a number of forms with either an electric or hydraulic motor drive. The motor and reduction gears may be mounted above or below deck. The anchor windlasses are built with wildcats (anchor cable lifters) only or in combination with warping heads, capstans and even constant tension mooring winches.

There are principally two types of anchor windlasses: 1) the horizontal, where the wildcat is on a horizontal drive shaft and lifts the cable vertically, and 2) the vertical, where the wildcat is on a vertical drive shaft and pulls the anchor chain horizontally. Both types are built as a single or double unit, that is, with one or two wildcats.

Windlasses are built with a hauling capacity of upward of 60 tons and a static load capacity of 300 tons or more, capable of handling upward of 400 fathoms of 4½" dia. stud link chain cable and a 20-ton anchor.

Fig. 2. Horizontal anchor windlass with two wildcats and two warping heads, anchor chains, chain stoppers, fairleads and top of hawsepipe. (Hyde Products, Inc.)

POWER, ANCHOR, CHAIN AND ROPE DATA*

	ANCHOR AND CHAIN				WARPING HEAD AND ROPE		ROPE CIRCUMFERENCE	
WINDLASS SIZE (no.)	CHAIN DIAMETER (ins.)	ANCHOR WEIGHTS (lbs.)	HP	MAXIMUM LINE PULL (lbs.)	HEAD DIAMETER (ins.)	ROPE BREAKING STRENGTH (lbs.)	MANILA (ins.)	NYLON (ins.)
5	1-7/8—1-1/2	2840- 4230	41	15000	18	27600	6	3-1/2
6	1-9/16—1-5/8	3500- 5020	48	15000	21	33100	7	3-3/4
7	1-11/16—1-3/4	4035- 6740	60	17500	21	35300	7	4
8	1-13/16—1-7/8	4630- 8330	72	20000	21	41900	7	4-1/2
9	1-15/16—2	5220- 9520	82	25000	24	46300	8	4-1/2
10	2-1/16—2-1/8	5820-10800	92.5	25000	24	50700	8	5
11	2-13/16—2-3/8	6740-13200	114	30000	27	57300	9	5
12	2-7/16—2-5/8	8330-16200	140	30000	27	63900	9	5-1/2
13	2-11/16—2-7/8	10120-19200	168	35000	30	70500	10	5-1/2
14	2-15/16—3-1/8	12000-23100	200	35000	30	77100	10	6
15	3-3/16—3-3/8	14200-27100	235	40000	33	86000	11	6-1/2

Note the difference in circumference of the Nylon rope as compared with the Manila.

*Hyde Products, Inc.

The accompanying tabulation shows the different sizes of the Hyde anchor windlass with the various power and strength characteristics up to 235 hp.

Each size is figured for maximum load. Horsepowers shown are for this maximum load. Horsepowers are calculated using hawse pipe efficiency of 60%, gearing and bearing efficiency 80%, hydraulic transmission efficiency 70%, total efficiency 33.6%, and chain speed of 32 fpm. All horsepowers are for two (2) anchors and 30-fathom chain, maximum size. Line pulls are approximately one-half the rope breaking strength as listed by the American Bureau of Ships, Section 24. Rope circumferences are taken from Navy Strength & Size Tables. Head diameters and lengths are taken from Navy Standard Gypsy Head plan.

On very big ships, especially those tankers which are approaching 500,000 tons and where larger windlasses and higher horsepower are required, using the single windlass permits a more ideal chain lead.

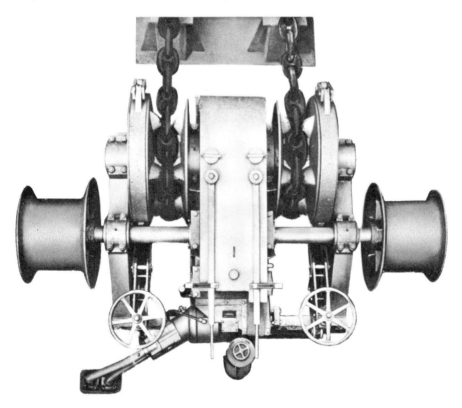

Fig. 3. View looking down on a double wildcat anchor windlass. Note the hydraulic fluid motor, brake operating handwheels, wildcat release levers. The small handwheel in the center is the control wheel for the hydraulic pump below deck. (Hyde Products, Inc.)

Fig. 4. (*Left*) Anchor windlass with gear case cover removed showing a chain of spur gears and the hydraulic fluid motor. Note the first two gears have herringbone cut teeth. Fig. 5. (*Right*) View of gear box (with cover removed) of windlass shown in Fig. 4. (Hyde Products, Inc.)

THE HORIZONTAL WINDLASS

The horizontal type of anchor windlass, Figs. 2, 3 and 10, is equipped with two wildcats and two warping heads. The windlass is capable of hoisting two anchors and their chains from a depth of 30 fathoms of water or one anchor and chain from a depth of 100 fathoms at an average chain speed of not less than 30 feet per minute. (For this requirement the motor may be run at 125% of its nominal rating at the start of the hoist.)

The windlass may be operated by one person. The gypsy or warping heads run all the time. The wildcats and warping heads may be operated in either direction. Clutches permit positive engagement of the wildcats and are centrally located with respect to each wildcat. Engage and disengage positions are identified on plates mounted near the clutch control levers.

The main gears are enclosed in an oiltight case necessitating a minimum of external lubricating points. Figures 4 and 5 show the main gears with cover removed.

Some anchor windlasses are equipped with completely oil-immersed worm drives and an open small-diameter spur gear meshing with a large-diameter main gear. Others are of the spur gear type but all gears running in oil, totally enclosed with only the main drive shaft leaving the reduction gear housing through oiltight seals.

When the windlass is powered by a hydraulic motor, the control of the windlass is through a handwheel which in turn controls the output of the electrohydraulic pump unit. When the windlass is driven by an electric motor, the speed is varied from zero to maximum in either direction by a multipoint lever-operated pedestal mounted controller.

Electrohydraulic Power

The power unit consists of a 1,200 rpm electric motor coupled directly to a variable delivery pump. The pump supplies oil to the fixed stroke motor on the windlass unit. Figure 6 shows the electric motor and variable volume hydraulic pump mounted on the oil storage and replenishing tank for the system. The control handwheel for stroking the pump can also be seen. This handwheel is for control of the pump output; the pump is located on the deck below.

An electric interlock switch is provided to prevent starting the electric motor unless the pump stroke control is in neutral position. A detent is provided in the control so the operator can feel the control being placed in neutral. There are directional arrows on the handwheel for *HOIST* and *LOWER*. Intermediate stroke points (quarter, half, three-quarter, and full) are also indicated on the control wheel nameplate.

The hydraulic motor drives the warping heads and wildcats through reduction gearing. A pressure-actuated horsepower limiting device designed to limit the demand imposed on the electric motor is provided in some cases; with this arrangement, regardless of the force exerted by the load, the motor will not run in excess of 125% of its nominal rating.

Fig. 6. Electrohydraulic pumping unit with variable volume pump. This unit is for operating hydraulically driven equipment such as the anchor windlass shown in Fig. 3.
(Hyde Products, Inc.)

Main Brake System

Each wildcat is fitted with a manual braking system operated by a handwheel. The brake bands can be clearly seen in Figs. 2, 3, 7, 8 and 10. Each brake is capable of stopping and holding the associated anchor and chain when hanging free at a depth of 45 fathoms and allowed to drop free for a distance of 15 fathoms with a five-fathom drift.

The two wildcat brakes are actuated through screw compressors. Five turns of the handwheel are required from full *OFF* to full *ON* as the range between first contact of the band and brake drum to full set tension of the band. The drum of the brake, being integral with the wildcat, transmits the forces on the wildcat directly to the bedplate and thence to the structure of the ship.

The brake bands are formed and fabricated for precision fit. The linings are riveted to the bands for optimum service and ease of refitting, if ever required aboard ship. Some manufacturers supply the winches with bare steel brake bands, making metal-to-metal contact for their braking force.

Some motors are equipped with slipping clutches set at about 50% above normal torque to protect them from sudden stresses. Disc or shoe type brakes held by powerful springs are provided to lock the motor and in turn hold the anchor. These brakes are released the instant the power is applied to the motor; they are operated either by a solenoid operated linkage or a simple clapper-type magnetic armature.

Spring-set, Hydraulic and Electric Brakes

On the horizontal windlass with the hydraulic drive there is a spring-set hydraulically released brake mounted on the pinion shaft (*see* Fig. 9) which stops and holds the windlass whenever the hydraulic power is interrupted. This spring-set, hydraulically released brake system is designed to function with the manual release mechanism. The brake sets when the pump is brought to zero stroke or if there is a loss of servo

Fig. 7. Warping head of anchor windlass. Also shown is the brake band on wildcat. (Hyde Products, Inc.)

power pressure. It is sized to maintain control of the anchor during hoisting or pay-out using power.

If the windlass is driven by an electric motor the windlass is furnished with an electric brake mounted on either the pinion shaft or the electric motor. The electric brake will perform the same function as described for the hydraulic brake. This brake is also spring-set.

Fig. 8. Details of brake handwheel and brake
linkage on anchor windlass.
(Hyde Products, Inc.)

Fig. 9. Details of spring-set hydraulically released
brake on a windlass fluid motor drive shaft.
(Hyde Products, Inc.)

Fig. 10. View showing a horizontal electric driven anchor windlass with two wildcats and two warping heads. The brake handwheels have been removed. (Hyde Products, Inc.)

Warping Heads

The warping heads handle Manila or synthetic hawsers, and a variable speed feature permits rapid recovery of line once free of the bits. The warping heads can be operated in either direction without rotation of the wildcats by disengaging the wildcat clutches. The heads rotate at all times when power is supplied to an hydraulic motor or an electric motor.

THE VERTICAL WINDLASS

The vertical windlass has its drive motor and reduction gear below deck with only the wildcat and capstan above the weather deck.

The advantage of this type of windlass is that the top side is very neat and shipshape. Having a low profile, the center of gravity is lower than the horizontal type windlass. This is very advantageous when using the larger size anchor chain found on the big ships of today. Also, the motor and reduction gears can be worked on at any time regardless of the weather.

Figure 11 shows a vertical windlass with dual shafts. The capstan takes the place of the warping head. The gear box and electric motor drive are shown on the deck below.

Braking and engaging the wildcats and the horizontal windlass are similar. Pedestal-mounted handwheels for operating the windlass are installed on the weather deck; also pedestal-mounted electric controllers, when electric motors are used.

Adjustable shaft couplings, between the drive shaft at the reduction gears and the above-deck assembly, allow for deflection of the deck.

The capstan runs all the time the anchor windlass is running, and the wildcat may or may not be engaged. If it is disengaged, it may be held motionless by its brake, or it may pay out chain by gravity at a speed controlled by its friction brake if necessary.

Fig. 11. Vertical windlass showing capstans and wildcats above deck. Note the reinforced deck fittings just below the wildcats. These are necessary to transmit the stresses caused by the anchor and chain to the ship's structure; this is also true of the stresses caused by the mooring lines. (Hyde Products, Inc.)

CHAPTER II

Miscellaneous Winches and Steering Gear

WARPING WINCHES

Although nearly every windlass, cargo winch and mooring winch may have a warping head mounted on it, there are also winches used exclusively for warping. These are often installed on the after deck where there are no cargo winches. This is particularly true of dredges.

The warping winch generally has two warping heads, one at each end of a main drive shaft. This main drive shaft may be as much as 25 feet long, supported at each end with an "A" frame outboard bearing. The main shaft is driven at the center by a motor through a worm gear, totally immersed in oil.

CAPSTANS

Capstans are designed for pulls upward of 20 tons and are driven from above or below deck. In the above-deck installation the drive motor and reduction gear are mounted on a common base with the capstan. In the below-deck installation the drive motor and reduction gear are mounted on the deck below making it easy to maintain under adverse weather conditions; only drip-proof motors are usually needed. With the motor and reduction gear below deck the area around the capstan is clear and shipshape.

One form of capstan has two diameters—the upper diameter, which is the smaller, is used for hauling in under heavy load; the lower part, with the larger diameter, is used for quickly hauling a slack line. This in effect is a two-speed capstan. There are both electric and hydraulic drives for the capstans. The electric motor drives are supplied for both AC and DC power to match the ship's generators. These drives will be considered later.

AUTOMATIC CONSTANT-TENSION
MOORING WINCH

The duty of an automatic constant-tension mooring winch is to continually supervise the tension on the mooring lines, maintaining the ship's position whether it be at the dockside, in canal locks, or in the harbor. The automatic constant-tension mooring winch shows its real usefulness in bad weather with heavy swells, fast running currents and change of tide.

In Fig. 12 are shown two constant-tension mooring winches installed with their drums fore and aft and their hawsers athwartship. This arrangement permits using the hawsers over either the port or starboard sides without going through blocks. Controls are installed abreast of the winches at the gunwale on both sides of the ship. These are start-stop push buttons, a single control lever, and a meter showing the hawser stress in tons.

This is an excellent arrangement for warping and shifting the ship at deckside, since it permits the operator a commanding view over the side of the ship both fore and aft, while having complete control over the winches.

The automatic constant-tension mooring winch may be operated either by an electric motor or by a hydraulic fluid motor receiving power from an electrohydraulic pumping unit. In either case, the motor is designed to maintain a constant pull on the hawser and to stall and hold the hawser at a preset stress. After this stress has been exceeded by a predetermined amount, the winch renders (pays out) the hawser.

When the winch hauls in a slack line, the speed may be increased to as much as 400 feet per minute. When hauling in a hawser under tension it will haul in until the tension equals the tension setting of the winch at which point the winch will stall and hold the hawser with a static torque equal to the preset tension. If, due to a change of tide or a heavy swell, the tension increases beyond the set point tension, the winch will pay out.

Fig. 12. View of two Constant-tension mooring winches. This is a typical installation with the mooring lines running athwartship. These winches are equipped with rope guards. (Hyde Products, Inc.)

Following are the characteristics of a 25,000-pound automatic constant-tension mooring winch manufactured by Hyde Products.

Maximum Pull	25,000 lbs.
Maximum Rendering	30,000 lbs.
Maximum Pull at 50 ft./min.	22,000 lbs.
Slack Line Adjustable Speed	0-400 ft./min.
Drum Capacity 1-1/8" Dia. Cable	600 ft.
AC Motor Rating	20 hp.

Figure 13 shows a constant-tension mooring winch in detail. Details of the electrical controls will be given later.

Fig. 13. Constant-tension mooring winch built by Lake Shore, Inc., with an electric motor drive. (Reliance Electric Co.)

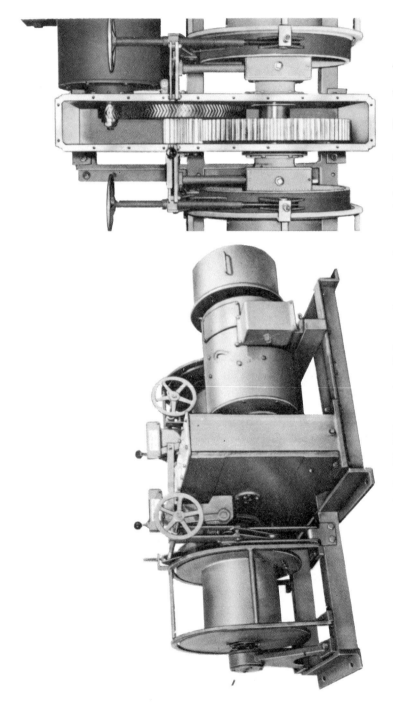

Fig. 14. (*Left*) Two-drum cargo winch with 50-hp. motor. Only one drum can be operated at a time. The other drum may hold a load with its handwheel brake. Note that the drum clutch operating levers are interlocked. Fig. 15. (*Right*) Same 50-hp winch as shown in Fig. 14 viewed from above with gear box cover removed. (Hyde Products, Inc.)

THE CARGO WINCH

Of all the winches aboard ship, the cargo winch has the most extreme and varied demands. It must, when fully loaded, change from its fastest hoisting speed to a crawling lowering speed. It must have a very fast hoisting and lowering speed and be able to set down a load of many tons very gently. It must operate at upward to 120 lifts per hour. This most versatile of winches is generally driven by a reversing type DC motor, although some cargo winches are driven by AC motors. The standard cargo winch is built to operate at speeds up to 250 ft. per minute for a five-ton load to, let us say, 80 ft. per minute for a 15-ton load. The speed varies according to the horsepower. Heavy lift winches are also built to handle 75 tons, and in special cases 250 tons. Though the cargo winch is designed to handle cargo exclusively, many are equipped with warping heads for mooring lines when shifting the ship, topping booms and hauling on preventer guys where no special winches have to be provided for these jobs.

Fig. 16. Single-drum 50-hp cargo winch. Electric drive with the brake on the end of the motor. The drum clutch lever is at the top; when the lever is towards the drum, the drum is disengaged from the motor but the warping head can still be used.
(Hyde Products, Inc.)

The cargo winch must have a high light line speed and a relatively fast rope speed when lifting the rated load. Also, when lowering the maximum load, the slowest, lowering speed shall be such as to produce a minimum impact on the landing of the load. The cargo winch is made with one or two drums and with or without warping heads.

The two-drum type shown in Fig. 14 has shift levers and positive lock-in lock-out type clutches. The drum brakes and clutches are interlocked to limit the operation of one drum at a time. The winch has rope guards designed to receive the lines from either direction.

The gears run in oil and are quiet. Figure 15 shows the gear box, clutch lever and braking mechanism in detail.

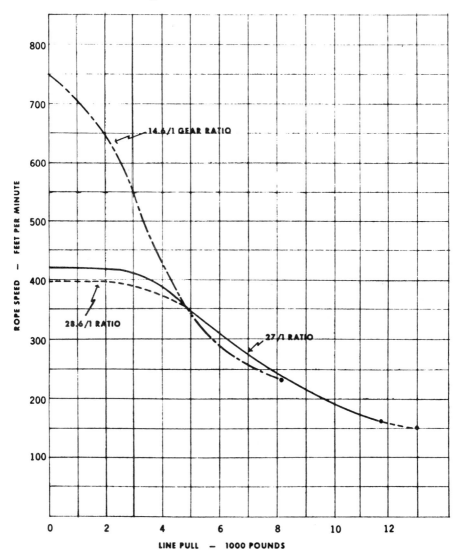

Fig. 17. Cargo handling performance curves showing the rope speed and line pull for different gear ratios for a 50-hp double-drum cargo winch.
(Hyde Products, Inc.)

Fig. 18. Single-drum heavy lift 100-hp cargo winch
with brake on end of motor shaft.
(Hyde Products, Inc.)

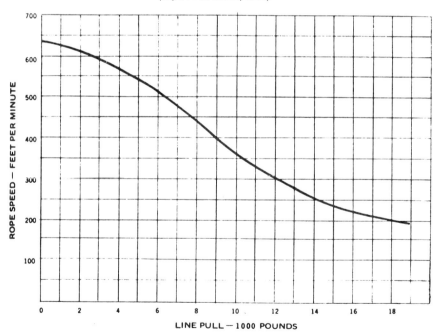

Fig. 19. Performance curves of 100-hp heavy lift cargo winch shown in Fig. 18.
(Hyde Products, Inc.)

The winch is fitted with a spring-set electric brake capable of safely stopping and holding any load within the capacity of the winch when the power is turned off to stop or when there is a power failure.

Figure 16 shows a single-drum winch of the same capacity as Fig. 14, but with warping head.

Both the two-drum and the single-drum cargo winches have 50 hp motors; both have a drum capacity of 685 feet of ¾" wire rope and can lift 11,750 lbs. at 160 ft./min.; both have an efficiency of 92%. Figure 17 shows the cargo handling performance curves for both of these winches. Note that when lifting 11,750 lbs. at 160 ft./min. the gear ratio used is 27 to 1.

Figure 18 shows the simplicity of design of the 100 hp single-drum heavy lift cargo winch. Its capacity is 9 tons at 200 ft./min. with a drum capacity of 1,460 feet of 1" wire hawser. The cargo handling performance curve is shown in Fig. 19. The gear ratio of this winch is 35 to 1. The slack line speed is 650 ft./min. The overall efficiency is given by the manufacturer as 92%.

Fig. 20. 50-hp single-drum cargo winch with electric motor and spring set, electric held brake mounted on end of motor. (Reliance Electric Co.)

Figure 20 shows external details of the brake and motor of a 50 hp single-drum cargo winch.

The heavy lift topping winch shown in Fig. 21 has a 50 hp motor and

Fig. 21. 50-hp heavy lift two-speed topping winch with brake on motor shaft and Hi and Lo gear change lever mounted on the gear box. (Hyde Products, Inc.)

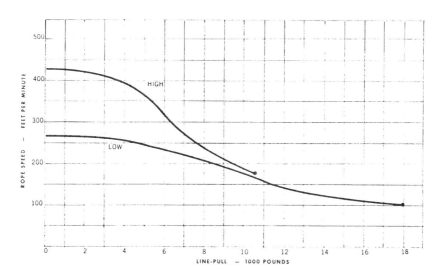

Fig. 22. Performance curves showing rope speed and line pull for high and low speeds for 50-hp topping winch shown in Fig. 21. (Hyde Products, Inc.)

two gear ratios—High and Low. The gear shift lever can be clearly seen at the end of the gear box. This winch will hoist 9 tons at 100 ft./min. in low gear; the drum will hold 1,620 feet of 1" wire. This is shown in the performance curve in Fig. 22.

Note the slack line speed is 260 ft./min. for the low gear and 430 ft./min. for the high gear.

Fig. 23. Hatch cover winch with Stearns electric brake mounted on the motor. (Hyde Products, Inc.)

Special application winches have appeared from time to time. One of the more recent is the hatch cover winch. Some of the specialized cargo ships such as ore carriers have side and end rolling hatches. Others have folding hatches which fold up in giant accordion fashion. All these hatch covers are heavy and require power to move them. This is the duty of the hatch cover winch. Figure 23 is an example of a modern hatch cover winch. Remote control permits the operation of the hatch covers from the bridge.

The mechanized hatch cover is not limited to the weather deck only but is found in the 'tween deck as a flush cover.

Simple compact low power winches will be found for handling the accommodation ladder, lifeboats, flexible loading pipes for tankers and other hoisting jobs.

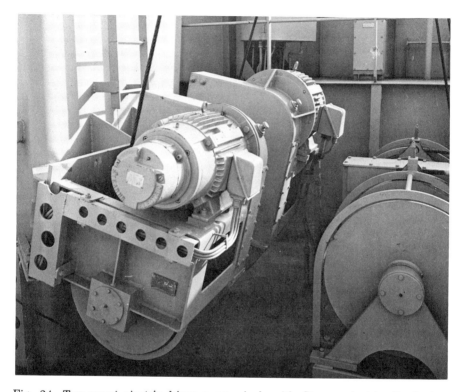

Fig. 24. Two-speed electric-driven vang winch with Stearns electric disc brakes mounted on the end of the motors. (Reliance Electric Co.)

Figure 24 shows a compact arrangement of two vang winches. Supported at the king post, these winches are equipped with Stearns magnet disc brakes for instant stopping and holding. They are for moving the booms into position by hauling or paying out of the vangs.

THE STEERING GEAR

There is probably no more rugged piece of machinery on board ship than the hydraulic ram type steering gear. It is built in two general forms: the compact type and the conventional type. They are quite similar.

Fig. 25. Hydraulic Steering Gear. Compact type. (Hyde Products, Inc.)

Fig. 26. View of partially assembled compact type steering gear.
(Hyde Products, Inc.)

The compact type shown in Figs. 25 and 26 has its hydraulic cylinders, rams and all other component parts factory assembled on a common bedplate and delivered to the shipyard as one modular unit. The bedplate is usually of all welded construction, designed and fabricated with sufficient strength and rigidity to adequately transmit the steering forces exerted on the rudder to the ship's frame.

In the conventional type, shown in Fig. 27, the major components are delivered to the shipyard ready for individual mounting (on shipyard-prepared foundations) on board ship. This allows for more flexibility in design.

The steering gear is capable of swinging from 35 degrees hard over right rudder to 35 degrees hard over left rudder, at an average rate of not less than 2-1/3 degrees per second. Under these conditions the ram and cylinder hydraulic pressure will not exceed the maximum design working pressures. Figures 28, 29 and 30 show close-up views of the trick wheels, the manually-operated ram stop valves, a detailed view of the tiller, and the Rapson slide, respectively.

Under normal conditions, that is, when the steering gear is in normal working order, the rudder is hydraulically locked at all times except when: 1) Normal rudder order is given by the control system; 2) Opening of a manual bypass valve; 3) Pressure in excess of normal relief valve settings (as may be caused by the rudder striking some object).

Failure of the electric or hydraulic power sources or control system power has no effect on the rudder lock. Hydraulic means are provided to prevent rudder overhauling.

Fig. 27. Hydraulic Steering Gear. Conventional type. (Hyde Products, Inc.)

Figures 31 and 32 show the steering gear arrangement for the single and twin rudder installations respectively. These are known as the Rapson slide type and the link type respectively.

Fig. 28. View showing trick wheels on conventional type steering gear.
(Hyde Products, Inc.)

Fig. 29. Details of Rapson slide on hydraulic steering gear.
(Hyde Products, Inc.)

An idea of the size of the larger of the single rudder steering gear units as shown in the former illustrations can be gained by referring to Fig. 31 and noting the overall length (L = 24′ - 4″) and the width of the cylinder base (W = 30″). The plunger diameter (D - 18″) and the distance from the center line of the rudder stock to the center line of the plunger R equals 45 inches. Where a double plunger is used, R becomes 2R—in this case, 90 inches. This equipment is capable of exerting a torque of 24,700,000 in. lbs.

In the foregoing example the maximum diameter rudder stock is 38 inches and the height of the tiller above the steering gear base is 36 inches. The pump supplies 127 gpm based on 2000 psi with a 60 hp pump motor. When a double plunger type of configuration is used, the torque pump and pump hp are doubled.

Fig. 30. Detail of steering showing Rapson slide in rudder hard-over position. (Hyde Products, Inc.)

In Fig. 32, the twin rudder installation, the torque of one size of installation is 18,300 in. lbs. for each rudder. In this arrangement L = 26′ - 4″, W = 30″, D = 18″, R = 55.

The weight of the rudder is carried on a thrust bearing and the tiller hub is split and keyed to the rudder stock. There are a number of different designs, but all must carry the weight of the rudder and all must provide for the secure attachment of the tiller arm to the rudder stock.

In the steering gear shown in Figs. 25-32 the hydraulic rams are outside packed and are guided by bronze bushings fitted in the cylinders. This packing does not usually require any adjustment during service. The ram stops serve as ultimate stops should the rudder take charge.

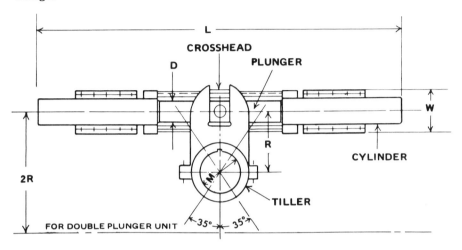

Fig. 31. Diagram showing single rudder arrangement with two hydraulic rams, tiller and Rapson slide. (Hyde Products, Inc.)

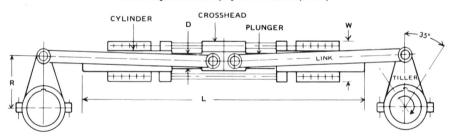

Fig. 32. Diagram showing twin rudder arrangement, hydraulic rams, crosshead and and linkage. (Hyde Products, Inc.)

There are two electric-driven hydraulic pumps and the steering gear may be transferred from one to the other. The pump motors may be started locally or remotely—in the steering gear room, engine room or bridge. The idle pump is hydraulically isolated by means of pilot-operated automatic blocking valves. Manually-operated stop valves are provided at each ram cylinder to prevent rudder movement in case of damage to piping.

The control of the steering gear from the steering gear room is by either of two trick wheels directly connected to the pump stroking shaft, as shown in Fig. 28. Mechanical helm indicators are furnished on the trick wheel stands in the steering gear space.

CHAPTER III

Hydraulic Pumps and Motors

Where it is desired to concentrate high power in a small space and to have smooth and precise control, the hydraulic fluid motor is particularly well suited. The characteristics of the hydraulic fluid motor lend themselves to handling such loads as the heaviest anchors and chains. Examples of this are shown in Figs. 3, 4, 5 and 9. The hydraulic fluid motors are constant-volume devices and the power output is controlled by varying the volume of oil input. Varying the volume of oil to the fluid motor is accomplished by using a variable volume pump.

The initial source of power for the pump is an electric motor powered by the ship's service generator. The electric motor runs continuously while the hydraulic system is in use. Two types of hydraulic pumps and motors, both positive displacements, will be considered: the vane pump and the axial piston pump.

The former (the vane pump) is constant volume and the latter (the axial piston pump) may be either constant volume or variable volume as required. Although the vane type may not be found on board ship in as many cases as the axial piston type, it is described in the following paragraphs.

In vane pumps, a rotor on the pump shaft carries movable vanes in slots in its periphery. Springs push the vanes outward against the contour of a surrounding cam ring. Rotor, vanes and cam ring form a pumping cartridge.

Fig. 33. View of vane pump cam ring and pump rotor. (Denison Division)*

The pumping cartridge is clearly shown in Fig. 33 and diagrammatically in Fig. 34. This cartridge is sandwiched between two port plates. Ports in these plates admit oil to the contoured areas of the cam ring, and permit the discharge of oil. As each spring-loaded vane follows the inner face of the cam ring, it moves outward as it enters the contoured area of the rings, drawing oil from the inlet ports. Having passed the inlet ports, the vane now travels up the slope of the discharge portion of the contoured area, pushing oil ahead of it. Here, as total

*Denison Division, Abex Corporation

area for the trapped oil is reduced, pressure is created and the oil is discharged through outlet ports in the cam ring at pressures up to 2500 psi.

In this type of vane pump (Denison) the vanes are said to be hydraulically balanced; that is, they are subject to hydraulic pressure as indicated by the arrows shown in Fig. 35, which balances the bearing load between the vane and the cam ring. This reduces the bearing pressure of the vane on the cam ring to that of the vane spring thus greatly reducing the wear of both the vane and the cam ring.

These pumps start easily at temperatures from -20°F. to $+120^{\circ}$ (-28.9°C. to $+48.9^{\circ}$C.). Servicing is very simple; the entire pumping cartridge can be replaced quite easily. Figure 36 shows a Denison Series TG single-stage floating cartridge vane type pump of higher power. This

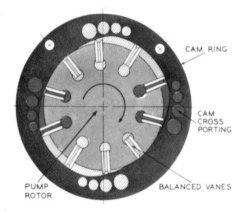
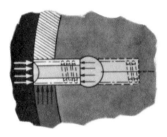

Fig. 34. (*Left*) Diagram showing main parts of vane pump. (Denison Division)

Fig. 35. (*Right*) Details of vane pump vane assembly. Arrows show balanced pressures. (Denison Division)

Fig. 36. Assembly—Vane type hydraulic pump; delivers 86 gpm at 2000 psi when 109.5 hp is applied to its shaft at 1200 rpm. (Denison Division)

series of pumps will develop 2000 psi at a flow of 86 gpm when 109.5 hp is applied to its shaft at 1200 rpm.

Figure 37 shows an exploded view of this pump. The pump consists of four basic components: (1) a housing with pad for pressure connections, (2) a pumping cartridge consisting of front and rear port plates, rotor, vanes, cam ring and springs, (3) shaft and seal assembly and (4) end cap with pad for inlet connections.

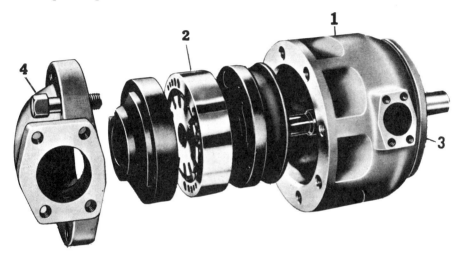

Fig. 37. Exploded view of vane pump shown in Fig. 36. 1. Main body; 2. Cam ring and rotor assembly; 3. Shaft; 4. End cap with suction flange. (Denison Division)

These pumps are equipped with a mechanical nose type shaft seal. The sealing is accomplished by the pressure of the spring holding a carbon ring which rotates with the shaft against a precision lapped surface on the seal face. This is shown clearly in Fig. 38. The shaft is supported by a ball bearing in the housing and a roller bearing which is located in the rear port plate at the end of the shaft. These bearings provide maximum shaft support which permits a greater side loading of the shaft.

A unique feature of these pumps is the floating pumping cartridge which is free to move axially within limits. To provide the necessary clamping force on this cartridge required for proper operation, the front port plate is pressure-loaded toward the cam ring. This clamping force increases with an increase in system pressure. A spring is used to hold the pumping cartridge together when there is no pressure in the system and for priming.

When the pump is in operation, oil enters the cap through the inlet connections, is drawn into the pumping cartridge through the rear port plate and is discharged through the front port plate and out the pressure port. The pump is internally drained at all times. Direction of oil flow cannot be changed in these pumps; however, the shaft rotation can be changed by indexing the cam ring to the dowel pin hole next to the arrow indicating the desired direction of rotation. The nameplate on the housing must be changed to match direction of rotation when cam ring is changed.

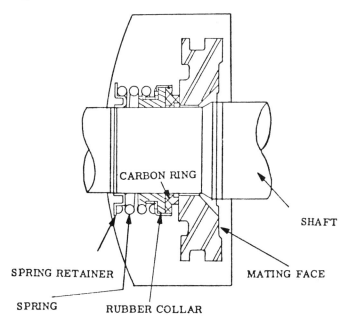

Fig. 38. Sectional drawing showing details of the shaft seal of the pump shown in Fig. 37. (Denison Division)

Referring to the section shown in the vane pump assembly drawing, Fig. 39, the following are the disassembly and reassembly procedures taken from the service literature for this pump. The various item numbers referred to in the procedure are those numbers shown in the sectional drawings (Fig. 39).

VANE PUMP DISASSEMBLY
(See Fig. 39)

Secure pump in vise with shaft extended down. Remove screws (1) in pressure and suction flanges (2) and (3) and "O" rings (4) and (5). Remove all screws (6) in end cap (7). Lift end cap (7) from pump housing and remove "O" ring (8), pull dowel pin (9) from cartridge. *Note:* All parts contained in floating cartridge must be handled with care to avoid damage to finished surfaces.

To remove floating cartridge, grasp the rear port plate (10) and pull outward. Remove snap rings (11) in (10) to remove bearing (12), press on outer race only. Do not press on rollers. The cam ring assembly can be removed by running two long screws in the threaded holes provided in cam ring (13). The rotor (14), vanes (15), vane springs (16) and spring guide (17) (no spring guide in TD Series) are removed as a unit. Place cam ring assembly (13, 14, 15, 16 and 17) on a clean flat surface covered with a clean lint-free cloth, push rotor (14) far enough out of cam ring (13) so that a large hose clamp or ring compressor can be securely fastened around the rotor (14) and over the vanes (15) and springs (16). After vanes and springs are securely held, rotor can be lifted from the cam ring. Slowly release the tension of clamp or compressor on the vanes and springs and remove them from rotor. The front port plate (18) is removed by running two long screws in the

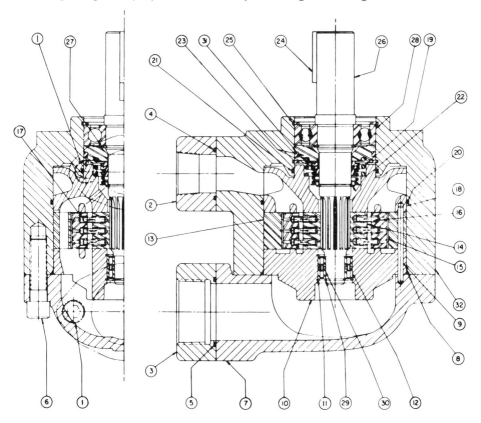

Fig. 39. Vane pump assembly drawing showing details of individual parts.
(Denison Division)

threaded holes in (18) and pulling plate out over splined end of shaft. It may be necessary to tap the outside of housing with a plastic or lead mallet while pulling on port plate. Remove spring (19) and "O" ring (20); "O" ring (21) can be removed now or after shaft assembly is removed. Remove retaining ring (22) which will relieve pressure on rotary seal assembly (23). From the seal assembly (23) remove spring retainer, spring, rubber collar and carbon ring. *Caution; handle carbon ring with care.* Allow mating face of seal to remain in pump for removal later. To complete disassembly, remove pump from vise. Remove key (24) and one of the retaining rings (25). The shaft (26) and all components attached can now be removed by pulling on the keyed end of shaft or pressing on the splined end. Remove snap ring (27), support inside race of bearing (28) and remove by pressing on splined end of shaft (26). Remove snap ring (29) and bearing inner race (30) from shaft. The seal mating face of item (23) can now be pushed out of the pump housing (32). Remove "O" ring (31) and, if necessary, the adjacent retaining ring (25) in housing.

VANE PUMP REASSEMBLY
(See Fig. 39)

Press bearing inner race (30) on shaft (26) and secure with snap ring (29). Press ball bearing (28) on shaft (26) and install snap ring (27) to hold bearing in place. Install the seal mating face over the shaft from the small end with the lapped face away from the bearing. Place heavy grease on carbon ring of seal and rubber collar, push these on the shaft from the small end until they contact the mating face. Next install the spring and retainer; then install retaining ring (22). *Caution:* Retaining ring (22) must be tight in groove; then install one (25) ring in inner ring groove in housing.

Place heavy grease on seal mating face and press shaft assembly into housing (32) by pressing against outer race only. Install second retaining ring (25). Insert spring (19) in groove provided in seal mating face. Insert "O" rings (20) and (21) in grooves in housing bores. Place heavy grease on "O" ring seals. Insert front port plate (18) into housing (32) by tapping lightly, but first index to proper position so dowel hole will line up correctly with dowel hole in end cap. Try vanes in all rotor slots to be sure there are no nicks or burrs to prevent free movement.

Lay rotor (14) face down on a clean flat surface. Install the springs (16) into the holes provided in the base of the rotor slots. Insert spring guides (17) in springs. Place vanes (15) carefully over the springs and into the rotor slots. Place ring compressor or hose clamp around the edge of the rotor-spring-vane assembly and draw up to compress vanes (15) into the rotor. Carefully insert the rotor-vane assembly into the cam ring (13). Be certain that the assembly is inserted far enough into the cam ring before the compressor is removed. Place cam ring assembly on shaft and against front port plate (18) so dowel pin hole with desired rotation arrow lines up with dowel hole in front port plate.

Install one retaining ring (11) in rear groove and replace bearing (12) in rear port plate (10) by pressing in place from the mating surface side of the port plate and install other retaining ring (11). Insert this assembly in pump housing over the shaft. Caution should be taken to properly line up rollers with the inner race before final assembly. Line up dowel pin hole in rear port plate (10) with dowel pin hole in cam ring (13) and insert dowel pin (9) through rear port plate, pumping cartridge assembly and front port plate. Install "O" ring (8) and cap screws (6), tighten evenly to recommended torque 60 ft./lbs. and reassembly is completed. After assembly, make certain that pump shaft can be turned by hand.

Several troubleshooting suggestions have been included as a guide to the ship's engineer should the need arise. This list, although applying to the particular pump under discussion, may be used as a guide when working on systems of similar design.

TROUBLESHOOTING SUGGESTIONS

Trouble	Cause	Remedy
External leakage around shaft.	Shaft packing worn.	Replace shaft packing per preceding instructions.
	Head of oil on suction pipe connection.	Sometimes necessary but will usually cause slight leakage.
Pump not delivering oil.	Foot valve in suction line.	These should never be used.
	Pump did not prime.	Bleed air from pump outlet (install needle valve for this purpose).
	Wrong direction on shaft rotation.	Must be reversed immediately to prevent seizure and breakage of parts due to lack of oil. Check flow and rotation arrows on housing.
	Tank oil level too low.	Add recommended oil and check level on both sides of tank baffle to be certain pump suction line is submerged.
	Oil intake pipe or suction filter clogged.	Filters must be cleaned of lint soon after new oil is added, due to fact new oil contains considerable amount. Check for water pockets around filter.

Trouble	Cause	Remedy
Pump not delivering oil (*cont.*).	Air leak in suction line.	Will prevent priming or cause noise and irregular action of control circuit.
	Oil viscosity too heavy to pick up prime.	Thinner oil should be used, per recommendation for given temperature and service.
	Broken pump shaft or rotor.	Refer to preceding service data for replacement instructions.
	Pump not delivering oil for any of the above reasons.	Check oil circulation by watching oil in tank, or removing plug in pressure line near pump.
Pump not developing pressure.	Relief valve setting not high enough.	Block winch operation, or oil circulation, and test with pressure gauge.
	Relief valve sticking open.	Dirt under pressure adjustment ball or cone. (See relief valve instructions).
	Leak in hydraulic control system (cylinders or valves).	Must be tested independently by blocking off circuit progressively.
	Free recirculation of oil to tank being allowed through system.	Directional control valve may be in open center, neutral or other return line opened unintentionally.
	Pump shaft sheared due to rotor seizure.	Disassemble and repair pump.
	Relief value venting.	Test venting circuit (if one used) by blocking vent near relief valve.
Pump making noise.	Small air leak at pump intake piping joints.	Test by pouring oil on joints while listening for change in sound of operation. Tighten as required.
	Air leak at pump shaft packing.	Pour oil around shaft while listening for change in sound of operation.
	Relief valve chattering.	Air being drawn into system at pump intake or pump shaft packing. (Check as above.)
	Porous pump casting.	Pour oil over pump to locate. Replace casting.
	Coupling misalignment.	Realign and replace shaft packing per preceding instructions.
	House breathing.	Increase housing bolt torque.

Trouble	Cause	Remedy
Pump making noise (*cont.*)	Partially clogged intake line, intake filter, or restricted intake pipe.	Pump must receive intake oil freely or cavitation will take place.
	Restriction pulled into intake cores (rags or paper).	Disassemble and clean pump. Remove head and clean carefully after valve plate bushings are removed.
	Air bubbles in intake oil.	Check thoroughly to be certain return lines are below oil level and well separated from intake.
	Tank air vent plugged.	Must be opened through breather opening or air filler.
	Pump running too fast (cavitation).	Check recommended maximum speed from descriptive literature.
	Too high an oil viscosity.	See oil specification sheet (use thinner oil).
	Filter too small.	Capacity may be adequate only when just cleaned and should have added capacity (normal size should be at least twice the maximum pump volume in gpm).
	Broken spring under vane.	Shut down and replace immediately.
	Pump drain line not below tank oil level.	Drain line must extend below oil level to prevent air being drawn into pump inlet.
	Cam ring not properly aligned.	Check cam to rotor concentricity with feeler gauges. Both lips of vanes must seal on constant radius portion of cam.

Clean oil is essential to get maximum service from the pump. Oil used in the system incorporating these units must be of the type recommended and should be kept free of dirt, lint, scale and other foreign materials which may damage the critical machined surfaces of parts within the pump. Oil filters are often necessary to insure having a clean hydraulic system, and should be installed. Filters should be used at the reservoir breather and the oil filter openings.

RECOMMENDED OIL SPECIFICATIONS*

Viscosity Range	150 to 300 SSU at 100° F.
Viscosity Index	90 or above
Maximum Viscosity at Starting Temperature	7,500 SSU
Neutralization Number	10 or below (when using new oil)

Additives—Recommended Rust and Oxidation Inhibitors and Minimum 0.6% W Zinc Dithiophosphate Anti-wear.

Caution: Temperature of the oil should never exceed 150° F. for most efficient operation.

The foregoing recommended oil specifications are given as an example of what is to be found in an equipment manufacturer's service manual. The proper service manual must be consulted before working on any piece of equipment.

DOUBLE VANE PUMP

This is a constant volume vane type pump with two pumping cartridges of different diameters on the same shaft. These pumps are built in sizes requiring driving motors up to 100 hp or more. The pumps have a common suction port and two discharge ports delivering two separate and different sized streams. This arrangement may be used to drive two

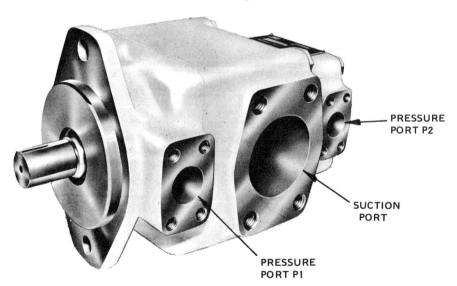

PRESSURE PORT P2

SUCTION PORT

PRESSURE PORT P1

Fig. 40. View of a completely assembled double vane pump. Note the large suction port in the center and the two high-pressure ports, one on each side. (Denison Division)

*Denison Division, Abex Corporation.

motors of different horsepower or the streams may be switched by control valves to operate the same motor at different hp output.

Figure 40 shows a view of the double pump. The common suction port is in the center housing with internal porting around the cam rings. The outlet ports (P1 and P2) are in the front mounting cap (large cartridge) and rear cap (small cartridge). Both outlet ports can be located independent of the suction port in any of four positions. The bearings are located at the drive end of the pump shaft and a seal is provided between the bearing and the end mounting cap which carries the discharge port (P1).

Figure 41 shows a cross section through a double vane pump.

Operation

In operation, oil enters the suction port in the center housing around the cam rings and enters the pumping cartridge at both sides of the cam rings through cast ports in the port plates. The oil is carried around to the discharge ports through the annular groove in the port plates and out the discharge ports in the end caps. The pump is internally drained at all times. The floating port plates move axially within limits so that hydraulic pressure can be utilized to counteract the internal hydraulic pressure that tends to separate the elements of the pumping cartridge after the pump is primed and delivering hydraulic pressure to the circuit. Light springs are used to hold the pumping cartridges together when there is no pressure in the system.

Changing Rotation

1. *P1 and P2 Cartridge.* To change the rotation of either cartridge, remove the cam ring and flip it over. Align the arrow on the cam ring with the arrow on the port plate indicating the direction of rotation.

There are many models of the double vane pump covering a wide range of combinations of double power output. Any combination can be built.

One pump of this design is rated as follows: The large cartridge referred to as P1 delivers 84 gpm at 2000 psi at a speed of 1800 rpm. This requires a shaft input of 105 hp. The small cartridge (P2) delivers 54.5 gpm at 2000 psi and requires a shaft input of 70.5 hp. The relative size of the two cartridges can be clearly seen in Fig. 43.

Figure 42 shows two views of the large cartridge (P1). The upper assembly is arranged for right-hand (clockwise) rotation. Note the small arrow. The lower assembly is for left-hand (counterclockwise) rotation as viewed from the drive shaft end.

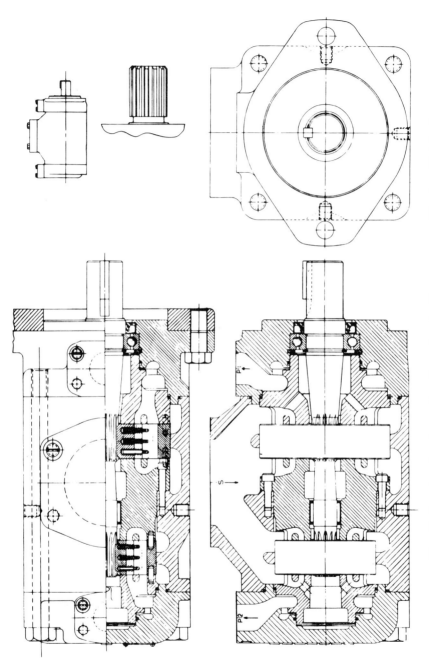

Fig. 41. Drawing showing section through a double vane pump. (Denison Division)

Operation

A. *Initial Starting*
    a. Be certain that pump is marked to operate in the same direction as the prime mover.
    b. Be certain that the oil used in the system conforms to specifications given by the manufacturer.
    c. Adjust the system relief valves for minimum pressure.
    d. Start the unit and allow it to build up to operating speed.
    e. Increase the system pressure to approximately 500 psi.
    f. At the start there will probably be some air trapped in the system. Purge the air from the system by venting at one of the hydraulic system valves. Operate the pump at low pressures (up to 500 psi) until it has been purged.

B. *Stopping*
Reduce the pressure setting for minimum pump delivery and cut the power.

C. *Low Temperature Starting*
When the temperature conditions are lower than the operating temperature ranges recommended in the oil specifications of the manufacturer, use the following procedure:
    a. Set the system relief valves for minimum pressure settings.
    b. Start the prime mover and allow the pump to reach idle operating speed.
    c. Allow the pump to idle until the oil is warmed within operating specifications.

OVERHAUL OF DOUBLE VANE PUMP
(Numbers in parentheses refer to Fig.43)
(See also Figs. 40 and 41)

General

Prepare a clean, lint-free surface on which to lay the internal parts of the pump. Thoroughly clean areas adjacent to the components being removed so as to minimize the danger of dirt entering the pump.

Disassembly—P2 Small Cartridge

1. Drain the pump.
2. Place the pump on a workbench.
3. Remove the screws (1) and end cap (2) and rear port plate. (Note position of end cap in relation to dowel pin (8).
4. Remove "O" ring (3).
5. Insert a 5/8-11 screw into the tapped hole provided in the center of the rear port plate (5) and remove the rear port plate and spring (6).

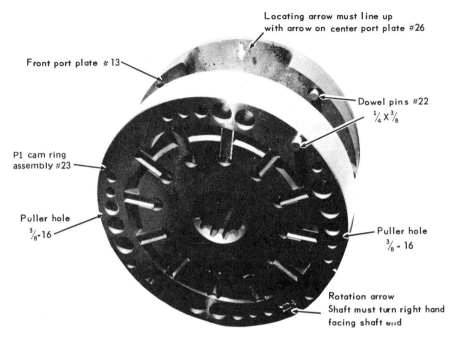

Locating arrow must line up
with arrow on center port plate #26

Front port plate #13

Dowel pins #22
$\frac{1}{4} \times \frac{3}{8}$

P1 cam ring
assembly #23

Puller hole
$\frac{3}{8}$-16

Puller hole
$\frac{3}{8}$ - 16

Rotation arrow
Shaft must turn right hand
facing shaft end

Above parts must be assembled in this manner in the mounting cap
and over the pump shaft for right hand operation.

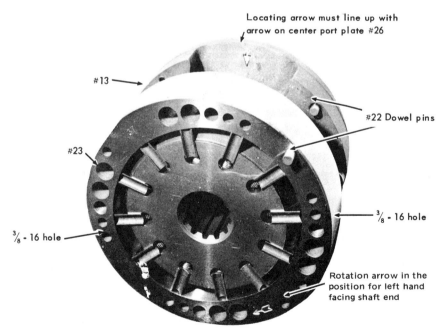

Locating arrow must line up with
arrow on center port plate #26

#13

#22 Dowel pins

#23

$\frac{3}{8}$ - 16 hole

$\frac{3}{8}$ - 16 hole

Rotation arrow in the
position for left hand
facing shaft end

Above parts must be assembled in this manner in the mounting cap
and over the pump shaft for left hand operation.

Fig. 42. View showing assembly details of cam ring for right and left hand
rotation. (Denison Division)

6. Remove the "O" rings (4) and (7).
7. Remove dowel pin (8).
8. Thread two 10-24 screws in the tapped holes provided as puller holes in the cam ring. Remove the cam ring, rotor, vanes, vane springs, and spring guides as a unit. (This is the cam ring assembly (9) P2 *See* Fig. 43.)

Warning: The vanes are held against the cam ring by tension from the springs in the rotor. If the rotor is pulled from the cam ring with no protection, tension from the springs will throw the vanes out in all directions. The repairman can be seriously injured by the sharp edges of the vanes.

Place the cam ring assembly on a clean, flat surface. Push the rotor and vanes from the cam ring far enough to secure a piston ring compressor over the vanes and around the rotor. After the compressor is in place, push the rotor and vanes the remainder of the way out of the cam ring. Release the tension on the compressor and remove the vanes, spring guides, and vane springs from the rotor.

Disassembly—Shaft End—P1 Large Cartridge

1. Remove bolts (10) from center housing (28) and mounting cap (11).
2. Separate mounting cap (11) and the attached shaft assembly from the center housing. (Notice position of front port plate (13) in relation to dowel pins (22) and cam ring assembly (23).
3. Remove "O" ring (12).
4. Thread two 10-24 screws in the tapped holes provided and remove the front port plate (13) from the mounting cap (11).
5. Remove "O" rings (14) and (15).
6. Remove the wavy washer spring (16) and snap ring (17) from the mounting cap.
7. Remove the key (29) from the shaft (20).
8. Push the shaft and bearing assembly out of the mounting cap.

Caution: Be careful not to damage the shaft seal.

9. Remove the shaft seal (21) by pressing on the back side of the seal from the front of the mounting cap, being certain not to scour the seal bore.
10. Remove the snap ring (17) from the shaft (20).
11. Remove the ball bearings (19) from the shaft by pressing on the inner face of the bearing.
12. Remove dowel pin (22) from (23). No. 23 is the P1 cam ring assembly. (Notice position of arrow on the cam ring in relation to the dowel pin and the position of the arrow on the center port plate (26).
13. Thread two screws to remove the cam ring assembly (23).

Follow the Same Procedure to Tear Down This Assembly As Used on the P2 Assembly.

14. Remove screws (24) and (25).

15. Remove center port plate (26) from the center housing (28).

Note: *Do Not Remove Roller Bearing (27) Unless It Is Worn and Must Be Replaced.*

    D. *Cleaning, Inspection, and Repair*

    1. Cleaning

Wash all metal parts in cleaning solvent (Stoddard Solvent or equal) and blow dry with clean compressed air.

    Caution: Dirt is a major cause of wear and pump failure. Cover all parts after cleaning to prevent dust and dirt from settling on them. After they have been cleaned, all surfaces should be coated with a film of hydraulic lubricating oil.

    2. Inspection and Repair

      a. Inspect the seal for wear and breaks. Replace a defective seal.

      b. Inspect all springs for cracks or permanent set. Replace a defective spring.

      c. Inspect bearings for wear or flat spots. Replace a defective bearing.

      d. Inspect the cam ring for wear. Replace a defective cam ring.

      e. Inspect the rotor for scores or marring on the wear face. Replace a defective rotor.

      f. Inspect the housing for cracks or other possible casting damage. Replace a damaged housing.

    E. *Lubrication*

No lubrication is required for this unit. The normal operation of the pump keeps parts adequately lubricated.

    F. *Reassembly*

      1. Press bearing (27) into center port plate (26) with stamped end of bearing against shoulder of the pressing tool. The near end of bearing must be set below the face of the center port plate (see manufacturer's specifications).

      2. Insert the center port plate (26) into the center housing (28) aligning the arrow on the suction ports with the large inlet port. Attach the center port plate to properly align the screw holes. Tighten securely and evenly, being careful not to cock the center port plate. Torque the 5/16" dia. bolts to 20 ft. lbs., and the 3/8" dia. bolts to 40 ft. lbs.

3. Assemble item (9) P2 cam ring assembly and item (23) P1 cam ring assembly in the following manner. See Fig. 43.
Place the cam ring, rotor, vane springs, spring guides, and vanes on a clean flat surface. Arrange the vanes side by side with the three spring holes up. Insert the vane springs in the vanes; insert the spring guides in the springs. Install the vanes with the guides and springs in the slots in the rotor.

Warning: Be certain that the heads of the spring guides and springs are started in the holes in each rotor slot.

Place a ring compressor around the vanes and tighten the compressor gradually until the springs and vanes are in the position they will occupy while in the cam ring. Install the rotor in the cam ring using a backup plate to prevent the vanes from sliding endwise in the slots and damaging the springs. If the vanes slide endwise, inspect and replace any damaged springs.

Warning: Be certain that the assembly is inserted far enough in the cam ring so that when the ring compressor is removed the vanes do not fly out of position.

4. Press ball bearing (19) on shaft (20) to shoulder and then install retaining ring (18) to hold bearing in place.

5. Press shaft seal (21) into mounting cap (11).

Note: Open face of seal must be toward inside of pump.

Caution: Special care must be taken to keep foreign matter from sealing lips of seal and to prevent cuts or abrasion of these edges.

6. Completely fill space between seal lips with high temperature grease. Press shaft assembly into mounting cap (11) from cap end of pump and bottom in bearing bore. Apply protective covering (may use tape or special metal tube) over keyway or spline end of shaft.

7. Insert retaining ring (17) in groove against bearing.

Caution: Retaining ring (17) must be fully seated in groove.

8. Install "O" rings (12) and (15) in mounting cap (11). Place heavy grease on both "O" rings. Install "O" ring (14) on front port plate (13). Place heavy grease on "O" ring. Position mounting cap and shaft assembly on workbench with coupling end of shaft extended down.

9. Place wavy washer spring (16) against retaining ring (17) and insert front port plate (13) into the mounting cap (11) taking care not to damage the "O" rings. Do not press port plate into position until porting is determined. The arrow on the front port plate (13) must line up with the arrow on the center port plate (26). For proper assembly of TDC pumps, see Fig. 42 for right-hand and left-hand operation.

10. Insert one dowel pin (22) in proper hole in front port plate (13). Check Fig. 42 again and place cam ring assembly (23) over pump shaft and over dowel pin (22). Place other dowel pin (22) in cam ring directly over the pin in the front port plate.

11. Place the center housing (28) and the attached parts over the splined shaft. Line up the arrow that is visible through the large inlet port with the arrow on the center port plate. Dowel pin (22) should be seated in the proper hole in port plate (26) when the arrows match.

12. Rotate the center housing (28), cam ring assembly (23) and front port plate (13) on the mounting cap (11) until the pressure outlet in (11) is in position for the desired porting. Install bolts (10) and tighten evenly. Torque in ft. lbs. as specified by the pump builder.

13. Check Fig. 43 and insert one dowel pin (8) in the proper hole in the small side of the center port plate. Thread two 10-24 screws into P2 cam ring assembly (9) and place over the shaft and on dowel pin (8) as indicated in Fig. 43.

    Caution: The arrows on P2 (9) and P1 (13) cam ring assembly must be pointing the same rotation or pump will not function.

14. Insert other dowel pin (8) in the cam ring directly over the first pin (8) that was inserted in center port plate. Place "O" rings (3), (4) and (7) in end cap (2) and rear port plate (5); apply heavy grease.

15. Insert spring (6) in P2 end cap (2) and insert rear port plate (5) in end cap. Place end cap and port plate on housing (28) and over dowel pin (8). The dowel pin will enter the correct hole in the rear port plate (5) when the arrows on both port plates (5) and (26) are in line.

16. Rotate the end cap (2) only to obtain the proper porting. Install bolts (1) and tighten evenly. Torque as specified by the pump builder.

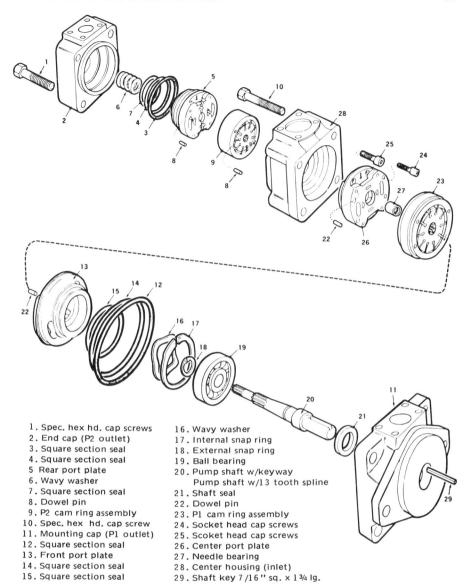

1. Spec. hex hd. cap screws
2. End cap (P2 outlet)
3. Square section seal
4. Square section seal
5 Rear port plate
6. Wavy washer
7. Square section seal
8. Dowel pin
9. P2 cam ring assembly
10. Spec. hex hd. cap screw
11. Mounting cap (P1 outlet)
12. Square section seal
13. Front port plate
14. Square section seal
15. Square section seal

16. Wavy washer
17. Internal snap ring
18. External snap ring
19. Ball bearing
20. Pump shaft w/keyway
    Pump shaft w/13 tooth spline
21. Shaft seal
22. Dowel pin
23. P1 cam ring assembly
24. Socket head cap screws
25. Scoket head cap screws
26. Center port plate
27. Needle bearing
28. Center housing (inlet)
29. Shaft key 7/16" sq. x 1¾ lg.

Fig. 43. Teardown and assembly sequence for a double vane pump.
(Denison Division)

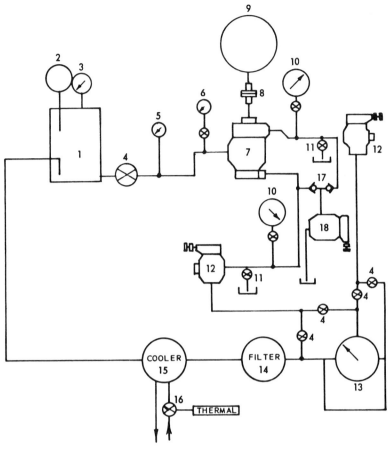

1. Reservoir
2. Air filter
3. Oil volume gauge
4. Gate valve
5. Oil temperature gauge
   (should not restrict suction)
6. Vacuum gauge (0-30 in. hg.)
7. Pump to be tested
8. Flexible coupling

9. Electric motor
10. Pressure gauge (0 to 4000 psi)
11. Air bleed off for priming pump
12. Relief valve (0 to 3000 psi)
13. Flow meter with inlet strainer
14. Oil filter
15. Cooler
16. Water valve with thermostatic control
17. Check valve
18. Relief valve (0 to 5000 psi)

Fig. 44. Schematic diagram of testing setup, indicating the major components used. Double vane pump shown under test. (Denison Division)

Testing Procedure for Dual Cartridge Vane Pumps
(Refer to Fig. 44)

1. a. Check hydraulic circuit and back-off relief valves to 0 psi.
   b. Check rotation arrow on nameplate.
   c. Open air bleed (11) until pump primes.
      Note: Pump and oil must be same temperature to prevent seizing. Soak pump in hot oil if necessary.
2. Start electric motor in cycling manner by alternately pushing start and stop button until pump primes.
3. Increase outlet pressure immediately to 500 psi on both circuits to permit pressure lubrication to rotors and prevent seizing.
4. Check flow meter for delivery on both cartridges immediately to see if oil is being delivered. If no oil is being delivered, shut off motor immediately. Check housing markings and motor rotation for correct assembly. Check pump inlet vacuum.
5. Run pump for minimum of 5 minutes at 2500 psi on small cartridge and 2000 psi on large cartridge.
6. Maintain oil temperature at 145° to 155° F. on 150 SSU oil.
7. Check deliveries at maximum rated rpm and at 0, 500, 1000, 1500, 2000 and 2500 psi on small cartridge and 0, 500, 1000, 1500 and 2000 psi on large cartridge. Deliveries should exceed minimum values.
8. Inspect shaft seal and housing for oil on air leaks.
9. Check pump noise level. If pump is noisy, check shaft seal for correct installation and suction line joints for air leaks.
10. If acceptable, remove from stand. Drain housing.
11. If not acceptable, see **Trouble Shooting Suggestions**. If trouble cannot be remedied, contact the pump manufacturer.

THE HYDRAULIC VANE TYPE PUMP/MOTOR

A very useful and versatile device, especially on board ship where space is always at a premium, is the hydraulic pump-fluid motor combination.

This dual purpose pump/motor is of single-stage vane type construction. It may be used interchangeably as a pump or fluid motor without adjustment or alteration. The pumping cartridge is designed with perfect radial balance making this multiple usage possible and also permits clockwise or counterclockwise shaft rotation.

Figure 45 shows a representative pump/motor completely assembled. As can be seen in Fig. 46, the pump/motor consists of three major subassemblies; 1) a housing, which provides a port connection and also acts as a support for the shaft bearings and shaft assembly; 2) a pumping cartridge, consisting of a rotor, vanes, springs and cam ring, and 3) a cap with a port connection.

This pump/motor manufactured by Denison is made in four basic sizes. Interchangeable cam rings in each of the basic sizes are supplied for changing the volume or motor torque. The major and minor inside diameters of the cam ring track are connected by ramps in regulating the displacement of the pump/motor. This arrangement of interchangeable cam rings provides a wide range of pumping rates and motor horsepower.

Fig. 45. View of a complete assembly of a vane type pump/motor. (Denison Division)

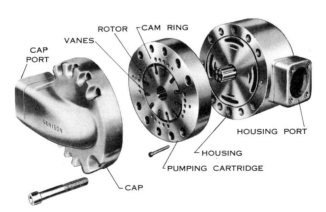

Fig. 46. Exploded view of the vane type pump/motor shown in Fig. 45. Note main components and simplicity of assembly. (Denison Division)

The alignment of the pump/motor is assured in the assembly when one of the flow arrows points to the desired rotation (*ROT*) arrow, as shown in Fig. 49. An exploded view of the pump/motor is shown in Fig. 47. The part reference numbers are listed in the legend for Fig. 47.

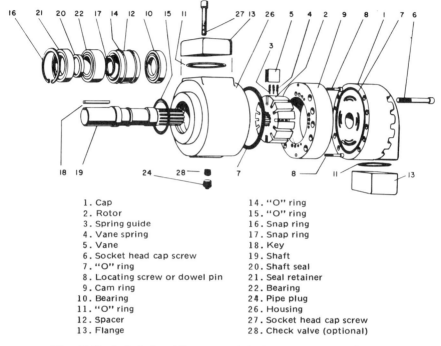

1. Cap	14. "O" ring
2. Rotor	15. "O" ring
3. Spring guide	16. Snap ring
4. Vane spring	17. Snap ring
5. Vane	18. Key
6. Socket head cap screw	19. Shaft
7. "O" ring	20. Shaft seal
8. Locating screw or dowel pin	21. Seal retainer
9. Cam ring	22. Bearing
10. Bearing	24. Pipe plug
11. "O" ring	26. Housing
12. Spacer	27. Socket head cap screw
13. Flange	28. Check valve (optional)

Fig. 47. Exploded view (diagrammatic) of vane type pump/motor.
(Denison Division)

Operating the Pump/Motor

The pump/motor will operate in either direction of rotation as a pump or fluid motor. When used as a pump, direction of flow may be reversed by changing direction of shaft rotation. When used as a fluid motor, direction or shaft rotation may be reversed by changing the direction of flow through the unit. A directional valve may be used to reverse the direction of shaft rotation when the unit is used as a fluid motor.

Draining the Pump/Motor

Normally, the pump/motor is externally drained, but provisions have been made for internal drainage under certain conditions. If the housing port is the low pressure port and never subject to more than 20 psi, static or surge pressure, the pump/motor may be internally drained. If the housing port is subjected to any pressure higher than 20 psi, it must be externally drained. This is done by removing outside drain plug (24) and connect to tank or another part of the system, subjected to the same pressure limits. For best results, the drain line should extend below the oil level.

Direction of Shaft Rotation

Direction of shaft rotation may be changed in two ways: 1) by flipping over the pumping cartridge so that the stamped letters, designating the type of pump/motor, on the other side of the pumping cartridge, are aligned to complete the model numbers (*see* Figs. 48 and 49); and 2) by reversing the piping.

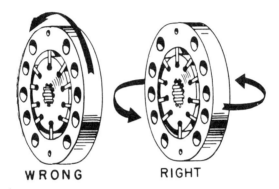

WRONG   **RIGHT**

Fig. 48. Showing the proper method of reversing pumping cartridge to produce a change in direction of shaft rotation. (Denison Division)

A series of arrows (*see* Fig. 49) are stamped on the pumping cartridge (cam ring) and housing, to indicate direction of flow and shaft rotation.

Two pairs of arrows stamped *Flow* are located on opposite sides of the pumping cartridge (*see* Fig. 49). Each pair of arrows points in opposite direction, to indicate direction of flow through the pump/ motor. Two raised cast arrows and the letters *ROT*, appear on only one side of the housing, indicating rotation of the shaft, when the pumping cartridge and housing are properly aligned, the arrows indicating flow will appear directly opposite the arrows indicating shaft rotation (*see* Fig. 48).

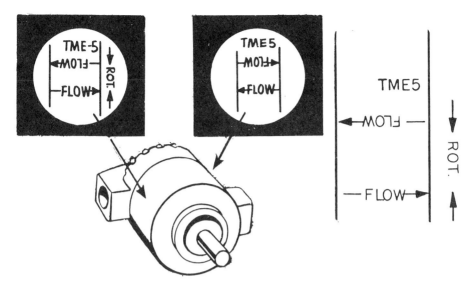

Fig. 49. Diagram showing markings to facilitate changing the direction of shaft rotation. See text. (Denison Division)

Disassembly

Refer to Fig. 47. If the unit is internally drained, remove pipe plug (24) and drain the oil from the unit. Remove the socket head cap screws (27), pressure and suction flanges (13) and "O" rings (11). Remove the socket head cap screws (6) and take off cap (1). Remove the socket head cap screws or dowel pins (8) and slide pumping cartridge off shaft (19). Be careful that rotor (2) does not fall out of cam ring (9) so the vanes (5) and springs (4) fly out of place. Remove "O" rings (7) from the sides of the cap (1) and housing (26). Remove snap ring (16) from housing (26) and remove seal retainer (21) with enclosed seal (20). Seal (20) is press fit into seal retainer (21). The two tapped holes on the face of seal retainer (21) are tapped for No. 10-24 N.C. screws as a service aid in pulling seal retainer (21) from the housing (26). Grasp housing (26) with both hands and with spline end of the shaft down, bump shaft (19) lightly on a block of wood. Once the shaft assembly is loose, remove it carefully from the housing. Remove inner bearing (10) and spacer (12). Snap ring (17) and outer bearing (22) may now be removed from the shaft (19).

Place pumping cartridge flat on a clean surface and pull the rotor (2) out far enough so that a hose clamp or ring compressor can be securely fastened over the vanes (5) and around the rotor (2). Once the hose clamp or compressor is in place, remove the rotor (2) from the cam ring. Release the tension on the hose clamp or ring compressor slowly so that the spring-loaded vanes (5) do not fly out of the rotor. After the hose clamp or ring compressor is removed, remove the vanes (5) and springs (4). Remove the check valve (28) from the housing drain hole. Before attempting to clean any of the parts, be sure that all "O" rings are removed.

Reassembly

Refer to Fig. 47. Be sure all parts are thoroughly cleaned and oiled before reassembling. Press outer bearing (22) on shaft (19). Install snap ring (17) to hold bearing (22) in place on shaft (19). Install the two "O" rings (14) on the spacer (12). Place spacer (12) over shaft (19) and press in the inner bearing (10).

Place heavy grease on all the "O" ring seals. Carefully push shaft assembly into the housing (26), do not damage "O" rings (14). Place grease on shaft seal (20) and press into retainer (21). Grease the "O" ring (15) and insert into housing bore groove. Push retainer (21) into bore of housing being careful not to damage the "O" ring (15). Install snap ring (16). If the pump/motor is to be internally drained, install check valve (28) and pipe plug (24) in housing (26).

Lay rotor (2) face down on a clean flat surface. Install the springs (4) into the slots provided in the base of the rotor slots. Be sure roll pins (3) are in place. Place vanes (5) carefully over the springs and into the rotor slots.

Place ring compressor or hose clamp around the edge of the rotor-spring-vane assembly and draw up to compress vanes (5) into the rotor. Carefully insert the rotor-vane assembly into the cam ring (9). Be certain that the assembly is inserted far enough into the cam ring (9) before the compressor is removed.

Place the two "O" rings (7) into the grooves on the sides of the cap (1) and housing (26). Be very careful that the rotor-vane assembly does not slide out of the cam ring at this point. Wash assembly in solvent, then oil thoroughly. Push rotor (2) on the shaft spline (19). Install the socket head cap screws or dowel pins (8) and tighten.

Secure cap (1) to housing (26) with socket head cap screws (6). Counter bores in the cap must line up with the heads of the socket head cap screws (6). For the convenience of piping, the cap (1) may be mounted in any one of two positions 180° from each other, without affecting the pumping action of the pump/motor. Be sure to tighten all socket head cap screws (6) evenly around the bolt circle. These should be tightened as per normal cap screw recommendations.

No shims or loose housing bolts are necessary in assembling this pump/motor, since all clearances are held by the close tolerances in machining the component parts.

The port flanges (13) are interchangeable in the two larger series pump/motors. The caps and housing of the small pump/motors are drilled and tapped for piping. The flanges with the large pipe tap should be used at the inlet for pump operation. Install the "O" rings (11) in the flange grooves on the larger series pumps and secure each flange to the housing with the socket head cap screws (27).

Fit key (18) to shaft (19). Replace check valve (28) and pipe plug (24) if the pump/motor is internally drained. The pump/motor must prime itself immediately when it is started again.

THE VANE TYPE FLUID MOTOR

As shown in a previous section, the vane type pump can be designed to operate as either a pump or a motor. Figure 50 shows a vane type motor known as series MIE built by Denison Co. This motor develops

Fig. 50. Complete assembly of vane
type fluid motor. (Denison Division)

123.33 horsepower at 2100 rpm with oil applied at 2000 psi; at this pressure the oil flows at the rate of 106 gpm. The motor weighs 110 lbs. and measures 9" dia. x 9" long, not including the drive shaft. This is very compact for so much horsepower. Figure 51 shows an end view and a longitudinal cross section of the pump shown in Fig. 50.

The maintenance and trouble shooting is virtually the same as for the vane type hydraulic pumps.

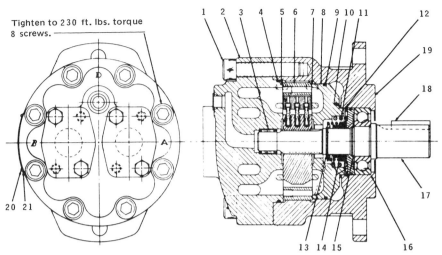

Tighten to 230 ft. lbs. torque
8 screws.

"D" is drain connection ¾-16 thirds.

Pressure applied to "A" will rotate motor
right hand (clockwise).

Pressure applied to "B" will rotate motor
left hand (counter-clockwise).

Rotation is always determined from shaft end.

Remove items 1 through 12 in the same order
as numbered. Press on coupling end of shaft
and remove items 13 through 17 as an assembly.

1. SHC screw	9. (s) Square section seal	16. Ball bearing
2. End cap	10. (s) Square section seal	17. Shaft w/keyway
3. Needle bearing	11. Spring (port plate)	Shaft w/13-tooth spline
4. (s) Square section seal	12. Int. snap ring	18. Shaft key
5. Dowel pin	13. Ext. snap ring	19. Body (housing)
6. Cam ring assembly	14. (s) Shaft seal	20. R.H. screw
7. Dowel pin	15. Ext. snap ring	21. ID plate
8. Front port plate assembly		

Fig. 51. End view and sectional drawing of vane type fluid motor shown in Fig. 50.
(Denison Division)

THE AXIAL PISTON CONSTANT VOLUME PUMP

The axial piston pump, as the name implies, has its pistons running
parallel to the drive shaft axis. The device is quite simple and efficient.
Figure 52 shows a complete assembly of this pump.

There is no crankshaft; the pistons are articulated in much the same
manner as the familiar "wobble plate" used in refrigeration compressors
where a slanting disk, turned by the drive shaft, pushes and pulls the
pistons in and out of the cylinders. Referring to Fig. 53, it will be seen
that the "wobble plate" is replaced with a stationary wedge-shaped disk
(32) centered about the drive shaft.

Mounted on the drive shaft is a barrel-shaped part (24) which fits
inside the body of the pump and is free to rotate with the shaft. The
barrel is bored almost its entire length parallel to the shaft to provide
cylinders for the pistons (27).

The piston assembly consists of hardened tool steel pistons, hollow on one end, and machined with a ball on the other end. A bronze shoe is crimped around the piston ball. The piston ball and shoe incorporates a drilling which carries pressure from the piston into a relief cut in the face of the piston shoe. This relief is a proper percentage area of the piston area to balance the piston axially so that there is lubrication between the piston shoe and the cam plate at all times. The rotating action of the pistons, while being held against the angular surface of the cam plate, imparts a reciprocation to the pistons, drawing oil in on the suction stroke and forcing oil out on the pressure stroke. The quantity of oil delivered by the pump is determined by the degree of angularity of the cam plate.

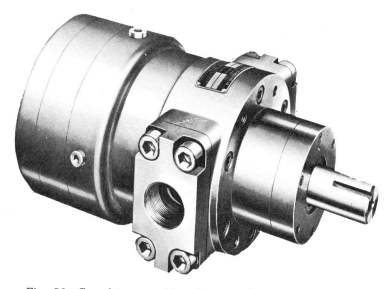

Fig. 52. Complete assembly of constant volume axial piston pump which delivers 35 gpm at 5000 psi when driven at 1200 rpm; this requires an input power of 113 hp. (Denison Division)

The hydraulic pump mechanism is enclosed in a housing consisting of three parts: The port block (9), the body (1), and the end cap (4). The port block incorporating the porting of the pump also houses the pump shaft assembly, which consists of two preloaded angular contact bearings spaced far enough apart to insure rigidity to the outboard portion of the shaft. A lip seal held in place by a removable seal retainer effectively prevents leakage around the shaft.

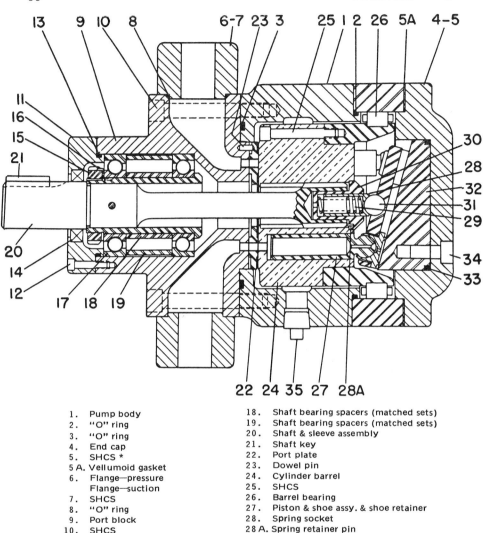

Fig. 53. Longitudinal cross section of the axial piston pump shown in Fig. 52.
(Denison Division)

1.   Pump body
2.   "O" ring
3.   "O" ring
4.   End cap
5.   SHCS *
5 A. Vellumoid gasket
6.   Flange—pressure
     Flange—suction
7.   SHCS
8.   "O" ring
9.   Port block
10. SHCS
11. Seal retainer
12. SHCS
13. "O" ring
14. Shaft seal
15. Shaft lock nut
16. Shaft lock washer
17. Shaft bearing (matched pairs)
 * Socket Head Cap Screws

18. Shaft bearing spacers (matched sets)
19. Shaft bearing spacers (matched sets)
20. Shaft & sleeve assembly
21. Shaft key
22. Port plate
23. Dowel pin
24. Cylinder barrel
25. SHCS
26. Barrel bearing
27. Piston & shoe assy. & shoe retainer
28. Spring socket
28 A. Spring retainer pin
29. Hold down spring
30. Spring retainer
31. Steel ball
32. Cam plate
33. "O" ring
34. SHCS
35. Sq. Hd. pipe plug

The port plate (22) is made of hardened tool steel lapped to highly polished surfaces on both sides. Arcuate shaped port openings mate with similar openings in the port block. The port plate is pinned in position and does not turn.

The cylinder barrel (24), or piston carrying member, is driven by a keyed or splined shaft. The valving of the porting is accomplished by the ported surface of the barrel rotating against the port plate, which has two arcuate shaped ports, one for suction and one for discharge. The bores in the barrel have small arcuate ports drilled on the same porting circle as the port plate and substantially of the same width as the suction and pressure ports. A blank unbroken surface separates the ends of the suction and pressure ports on the port plate, and this constitutes the cutoff between pressure and suction. The cylinder barrel is held in proper abutment with the port plate by the spring hold-down assembly which fits in the splined end shaft and also holds the pistons out against the cam plate on the suction stroke.

Figure 52 shows the complete assembly of a Denison Series 800 constant volume type pump. One model of this pump will deliver 34.5 gpm at 5000 psi when 113 hp is applied to its drive shaft at 1200 rpm.

Figure 53 is a drawing showing a longitudinal cross section through the same pump; looking at the drawing we can see the cam plate (32), held in place by socket head screws (34), the shoes which slide on the cam plate also carry the socket into which the ball end of the hollow piston (27) fits, and the shoe retaining ring. The port plate (22) can be seen connecting the *head* end of the cylinders to the suction and discharge chambers which in turn are connected to the external piping.

THE AXIAL PISTON VARIABLE VOLUME TYPE PUMP

The variable volume characteristics of the axial piston pump are made possible by varying the piston stroke continuously or in steps, from zero to maximum.

Figure 54 shows the complete assembly of an axial piston variable volume pump. The pump shown is designed to operate at pressures up to 5000 psi. Power applied to the shaft turns the rotating assembly (barrel and bearing assembly, piston and shoe assembly and attached parts) creating the pumping action.

Fig. 54. Complete assembly of a variable volume axial piston pump.
(Denison Division)

In the place of the fixed cam plate as in the constant volume pump there is a circular plate mounted on a heavy member called a hanger. This circular plate is called the index plate. The piston strokes are changed by raising the hanger above center to increase the volume. The volume is decreased by returning the hanger to center. The raising and lowering of the hanger cause the tilting of the index plate. This simulates the effect of a cam plate. For design reasons which give improved operation, a free floating circular flat plate called a "creep" plate is inserted between the index plate and the piston shoe assembly. As the index plate tilts, so does the creep plate which changes the cam effect;

this in turn changes the length of the stroke of the pistons. These details can be clearly seen in Figs. 55 and 56.

The thrust of the pistons is balanced by the admission of pressure through a drilling in the piston into an area in the surface of the piston shoe that contacts the creep plate. This area is slightly less than the effective piston area, which results from the shoe being supported on an oil film at all times. The cylinder barrel is supported in a conventional type port plate in which are machined support areas hydraulically balancing this portion of the pump.

The radial load created by the angle of the creep plate is supported by a precision roller bearing which is placed at the point of average load, effectively balancing all radial forces. The cylinder barrel is driven by a spline, the center of which is located at the same point of average load resulting in the balancing of all driving forces.

The variable delivery controls are bolted to the pump housing in easily removable units. A four-hole square flange for this purpose can be seen on top and to the rear of the pump (see Fig. 54). All working parts are submerged in a bath of oil. Due to the simplicity of design, maintenance and service problems are greatly minimized. Figure 57 shows an exploded view of this pump. The various parts can be easily identified. Refer also to Fig. 59, which is a cutaway view of the whole pump assembly with pressure compensated handwheel volume control.

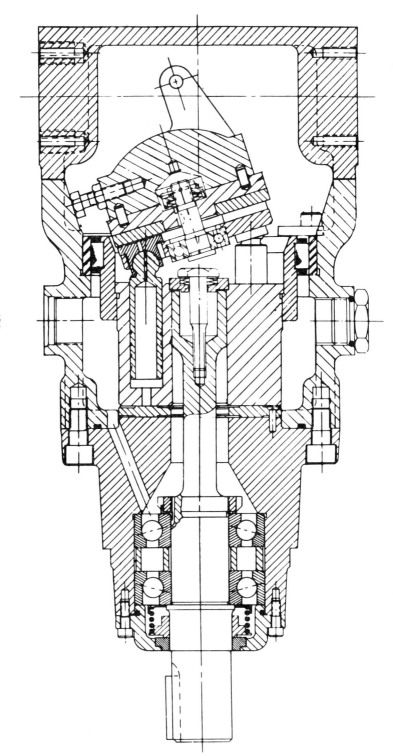

TOP

Fig. 55. Vertical longitudinal cross section of the variable volume axial piston pump shown in Fig. 54. (Denison Division)

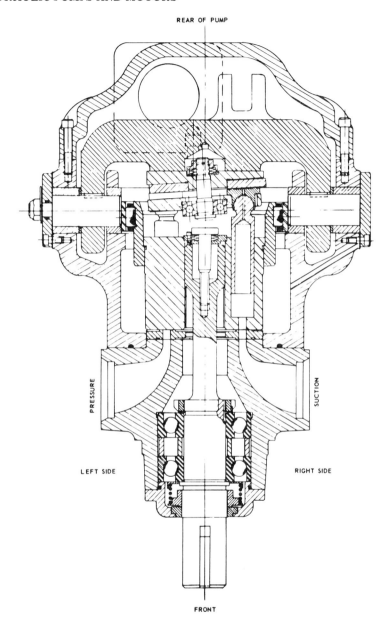

Fig. 56. Horizontal longitudinal cross section of the variable volume axial piston pump shown in Fig. 54. (Denison Division)

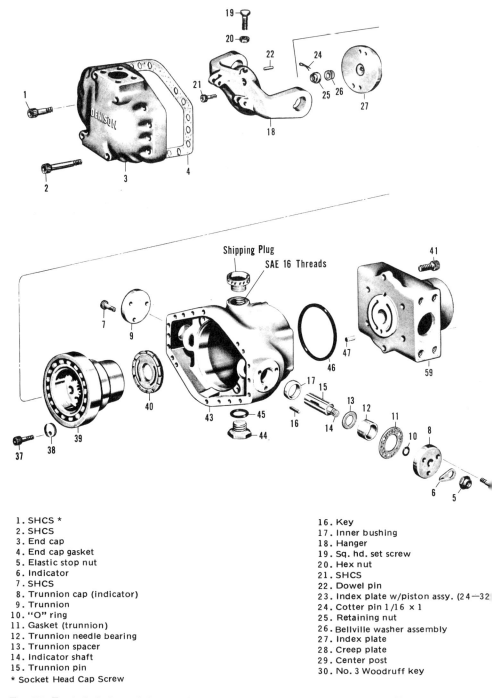

Shipping Plug

SAE 16 Threads

1. SHCS *
2. SHCS
3. End cap
4. End cap gasket
5. Elastic stop nut
6. Indicator
7. SHCS
8. Trunnion cap (indicator)
9. Trunnion
10. "O" ring
11. Gasket (trunnion)
12. Trunnion needle bearing
13. Trunnion spacer
14. Indicator shaft
15. Trunnion pin
* Socket Head Cap Screw

16. Key
17. Inner bushing
18. Hanger
19. Sq. hd. set screw
20. Hex nut
21. SHCS
22. Dowel pin
23. Index plate w/piston assy. (24—32
24. Cotter pin 1/16 × 1
25. Retaining nut
26. Bellville washer assembly
27. Index plate
28. Creep plate
29. Center post
30. No. 3 Woodruff key

Fig. 57. Exploded view of the variable volume axial piston pump shown in Figs. 54 to 56.
(Denison Division)

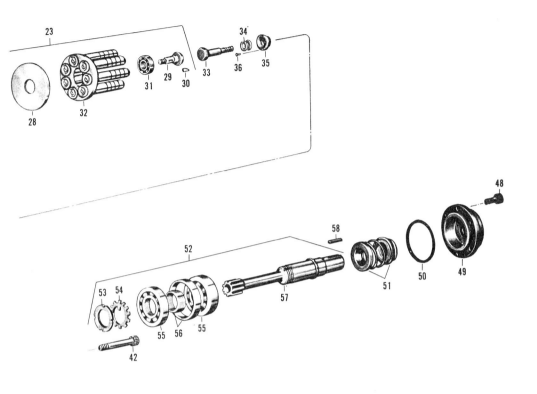

31. Ball bearing	45. "O" ring
32. Piston & shoe assy. w/retainer	46. "O" ring
33. Holddown screw	47. Port plate pin
34. Bellville washer assembly	48. SHCS
35. Spring retainer	49. Shaft seal retainer
36. SHCS	50. "O" ring
37. SHCS	51. Shaft seal assembly
38. Barrel stop	52. Shaft & bearing assy. (53—57)
39. Barrel & bearing assembly	53. Lock nut
40. Right-hand port plate (CW)	54. Lock washer
Left-hand port plate (CCW)	55. Shaft bearing (matched pair)
41. SHCS	56. Bearing spacer assembly
42. SHCS	57. Pump shaft
43. Hanger housing	58. Shaft key
44. Hex plug	59. Port block

Right side of Fig. 57.

VARIABLE VOLUME DELIVERY CONTROL

There are a number of different types of variable volume controls but they all have the same duty, which is positioning the hanger so that the cam plate is at the proper angle. The different types in Figs. 58A to 58F are described as follows:

Handwheel Control

Figure 58A—A handwheel which positions the pump cam plate affords manual regulation of pump volume. An indicator shows when it is set for quarter, half, three-quarter or full delivery. An adjustable minimum-volume control device is also provided.

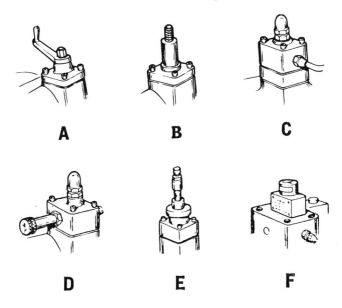

Fig. 58A-F. Views showing the various methods of operating the variable volume control mechanism. (Denison Division)

Stem Control

Figure 58B—A short stem, mechanically linked to the driven equipment, changes the angle of the pump's cam plate and regulates volume to meet varying volume demands. An adjustable minimum-volume control device is also provided.

Hydraulic Cylinder Control

Figure 58C—Similar to stem control, except that the angle of the pump's cam plate is changed hydraulically instead of mechanically to regulate pump volume. It may be actuated by pilot lines from any part of the hydraulic system, or by external sources and does not depend upon working pressure of the hydraulic system for operation. Maximum and minimum volume may also be adjusted.

Pressure Compensator Control

Figure 58D—Provides automatic regulation of pump volume to pressure demands. The pump delivers full volume when working at less than, or to achieve, preset maximum system pressure. Once that pressure is attained, the pump delivers only the volume required to maintain it. This is ideal where system pressure requirements, such as those in holding operations, are encountered. Horsepower input need only be that required to meet immediate pressure and volume demands. Maximum pressure may be preset by means of a knurled knob adjustment. Pumps with this control may also be equipped with Handwheel Control, for quick adjustment of maximum volume to be delivered, and are used for anchor windlass and winch control.

Servo Control

Figure 58E—Affords infinite variation of pump volume. It consists of two elements operating either in line or axially and requiring a minimum signal and physical effort. The first of these elements is the signal transmitting stem, the second is the error-detecting and servo piston. A linear or rotary signal to the stem moves a control spool to direct hydraulic fluid to top or bottom of the control piston which, in turn, positions the pump cam plate. When the signal is removed, the control piston automatically closes porting communication with the spool and becomes stationary.

Electrohydraulic Servo Control

Figure 58F—A two-stage electrohydraulic flow valve which transforms a low-power electrical input signal into hydraulic pressure output for controlling position of the pump's cam plate. In doing so, it shortens or lenghtens the stroke of the pumping pistons to increase or decrease pump output volume. A cam-angle feedback potentiometer, deposited plastic film type with a useful service life of a hundred million cycles, is provided. The electrical input signal source is usually a potentiometer. Hydraulic pressure is derived from a built-in servo pressure pump, or an external one. This system may be used with steering gear systems.

Figure 59 shows a cutaway view of a pressure compensated handwheel control mounted on an axial piston variable volume pump. Starting at the top of the picture and working down is the handwheel's locking lever. Horizontally arranged across the control line up is the pressure compensating device. Below this is the control piston (marked piston) which controls the hanger. Secured to the hanger is the index plate; then follows the cam or creep plate. After this, to the left, are the barrel assembly and the pistons with ball and socket shoes. Note the large double bearing which carries the cantilever weight of the barrel and pistons.

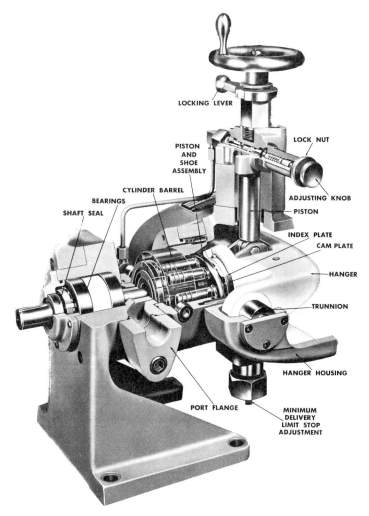

Fig. 59. Cutaway view of a variable volume axial piston pump showing detail of hanger and pressure compensated handwheel control. (Denison Division)

Description and Operation

The operation of the handwheel pressure compensator type pump is really a combination of two pump controls. The handwheel adjustment limits the maximum amount of volume which can be delivered by the pumps, and the compensator automatically reduces the volume, once

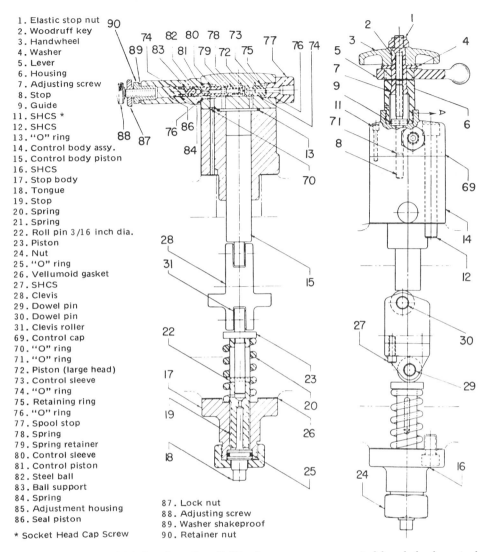

1. Elastic stop nut
2. Woodruff key
3. Handwheel
4. Washer
5. Lever
6. Housing
7. Adjusting screw
8. Stop
9. Guide
11. SHCS *
12. SHCS
13. "O" ring
14. Control body assy.
15. Control body piston
16. SHCS
17. Stop body
18. Tongue
19. Stop
20. Spring
21. Spring
22. Roll pin 3/16 inch dia.
23. Piston
24. Nut
25. "O" ring
26. Vellumoid gasket
27. SHCS
28. Clevis
29. Dowel pin
30. Dowel pin
31. Clevis roller
69. Control cap
70. "O" ring
71. "O" ring
72. Piston (large head)
73. Control sleeve
74. "O" ring
75. Retaining ring
76. "O" ring
77. Spool stop
78. Spring
79. Spring retainer
80. Control sleeve
81. Control piston
82. Steel ball
83. Ball support
84. Spring
85. Adjustment housing
86. Seal piston
87. Lock nut
88. Adjusting screw
89. Washer shakeproof
90. Retainer nut

* Socket Head Cap Screw

Fig. 60. Elevation (right) and section (left) of pressure compensated handwheel control for a variable volume axial piston pump. (Denison Division)

pressure has started to build up. As the pressure increases in the system, the compensator valve shifts. The flow from the compensator valve is applied directly against a piston, pressing this against the hanger mechanism, reducing the angle of the cam plate. The greater the pressure, the greater distance the hanger is depressed, reducing the volume but maintaining pressure. The volume will continue to reduce until the bottom stop (located on opposite side of pump housing) is encountered. This minimum stop is used only when it is not desirable to go to "O" volume delivery. The adjustment which decides when the pump is to decrease its volume is the knurled knob located on top of the pump housing. Always be certain that after adjustment the knurled locknut is hand-tight. The minimum adjustment stop is adjusted in much the same manner.

Figure 60 shows an elevation (on the right) and section (on the left) of a pressure compensated handwheel control assembly. Great care should be taken to keep all parts and the oil absolutely free from any foreign matter.

The builders of hydraulic equipment keep strict surveillance over the cleanliness of the equipment at all times and particularly during assembly. Many surfaces are lapped to a fine finish and the slightest scratch will impair the operation of the equipment. Scratches should be removed by lapping before reassembly if necessary. Use manufacturer's recommendation for lapping compound. Remove all pressure before going into the system for any reason, such as repair or disassembly, etc.

Note: If any of the connecting piping is to be replaced because of damage or other reasons, do not use galvanized pipe for this purpose.

Figure 61 shows a high speed axial piston variable volume pump with pressure compensated handwheel control. Although this pump is less than 12" across the main body, it receives an input of 60 hp delivering 30 gpm at 3500 psi.

When the handwheel control is used on board ship for pumps that are below deck, as in cases of the anchor windlass, etc., the handwheel (as seen in Figs. 59 and 61) is removed and an extension rod is installed, thus providing control from the deck above. This can also be seen in Figs. 3 and 6.

Fig. 61. High speed variable volume axial piston pump. Maximum operating condition: speed 3750 rpm, pressure 5000 psi, delivering 15 gpm at 5000 psi, or 30 gpm at 3000 psi with an input of 60 hp. (Denison Division)

PUMPING UNITS

These units are each comprised of an electric motor drive, a pump and a reservoir type base, all assembled as a package unit. They are designed to meet the standards set by the JIC (Joint Industry Conference). Figure 62 is a typical higher powered hydraulic pumping unit. These units are built having motors up to 200 hp at 1200 or 1800 rpm and operating axial piston pumps up to 5000 psi.

Fig. 62. View of an electric-driven pumping unit.
(Denison Division)

CHAPTER IV

The Axial Piston Type Fluid Motor

The design of the axial piston, constant displacement fixed stroke fluid motor is quite similar to the axial piston constant volume pump. This can be seen in Fig. 63.

How It Works

Oil under pressure enters the motor, passes through the inlet port of the port plate and into those cylinders of the cylinder barrel which are at that moment opposite that port. As oil enters each cylinder, it builds up pressure in and against a hollow piston and its hydraulically-balanced piston shoe—pressure which is transmitted against the sloping face of the pump's cam plate. The angular reaction of shoe and piston

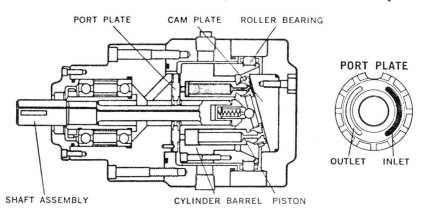

Fig. 63. Diagram of axial piston constant displacement fluid motor.
(Denison Division)

to this pressure causes them to seek the lower side of the sloping cam plate, both piston and shoe moving outward. In doing so, they impart radial force to the cylinder barrel, causing it to turn and creating output torque of the motor. As the barrel turns and the shoe descends the sloping cam plate, its piston is forced outward. As it comes opposite the outlet port in the port plate, its oil passes through that port and from the motor. Meanwhile, the following pistons are receiving oil under pressure, seeking the lower side of the cam plate, and continuing the turning movement of the cylinder barrel and its shaft. Thus, torque of the motor depends upon pressure of the oil, speed upon its volume—both may be regulated.

Many of the hydraulic motors are identical to the constant volume hydraulic pumps of the same manufacture and similar capacity;

70

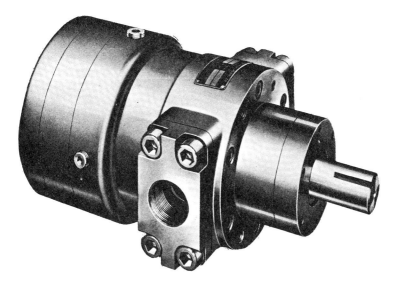

Fig. 64. Complete assembly of an axial piston constant displacement
fluid motor. (Denison Division)

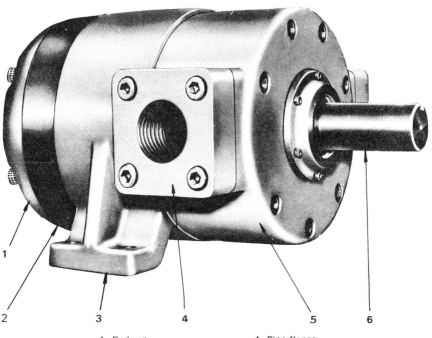

1. End cap   4. Pipe flange
2. Bearing and barrel assembly   5. Port block
3. Motor body   6. Output shaft

Fig. 65. Axial piston, constant displacement (fixed stroke) fluid motor. This
motor delivers 310 hp at 1500 rpm. (Denison Division)

compare Fig. 64 with Fig. 52. The motor in Fig. 64 is a Denison 800 series, delivering 180 hp at 2000 rpm with a flow of 61.7 gpm at 5000 psi.

The following is a description of a 310 hp, 1500 rpm axial piston constant displacement, fixed stroke fluid motor, as shown in Figs. 65 and 66.

This is a hydraulic motor of the axial piston type. Driving action is accomplished by the high pressure inlet oil forcing the pistons out, rotating the barrel and shaft assemblies. The piston and shoe retainer assembly (8, Fig. 66) is held in contact with the cam plate (5) by spring (13). As the shaft and bearing assembly (40) is rotated by the cylinder barrel (19), the pistons (10) in the piston and shoe retainer (9) move axially in and out of the cylinder barrel chambers as guided by the inclination of the cam plate (5). Each piston moves axially inward during one-half revolution of the shaft and axially outward during the other half revolution. As each piston moves axially inward, oil is expelled from the cylinder cavity through one of two arcuate ports in the port plate (28).

All piping should be of adequate size and strength to assure free flow at the pressures involved. All system piping must be clean in accordance with Military Specification MIL-C-17795 before the pump is connected. Piping workmanship must be accurate in order to eliminate any undue strain on the pump when tightening flange bolts.

The following gives the recommended safe steady state operating conditions of oil viscosity and temperature for the motor. The safe viscosity range is 240 to 260 SSU (Saybolt Seconds Universal).

Operating oil temperature range (Fahrenheit)	MIL-L-17331 Oil Symbol
60°–120°	2190TEP

Initial Starting

Refer to Figs. 66 and 67. Before the motor is put into operation, remove the cap screws (22) and tank-return flange (23). Then break the line into the motor housing to make certain that the motor is filled to the top of the tank-return flange boss of the motor housing.

When replacing the tank-return flange (23), make sure the "O" ring (24) is nested in the groove of the tank-return flange boss. With "O" ring (24) in place, replace tank-return flange (23) and secure in place with screws (22). After the hydraulic system and motor have been filled with the proper oil, it should be purged completely of air. Adjust the system relief valves for minimum pressure. Start the unit and allow it to build up operating speed; increase pressure to approximately 500 psi. Check the unit for undue noise and system leaks. At the start there will

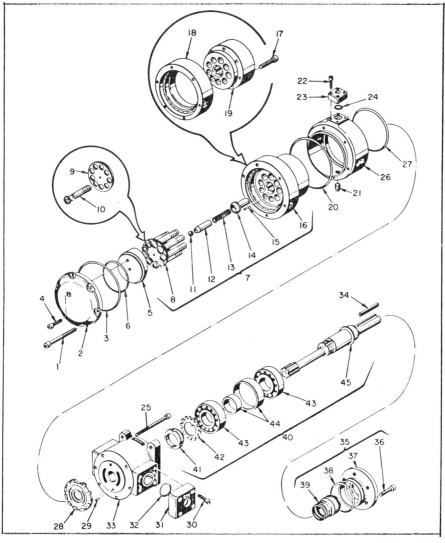

1. Cap screw	16. Bearing and barrel assy.
2. End cap	17. Cap screw
3. "O" ring	18. Rollway bearing
4. Cap screw	19. Cylinder barrel
5. Cam plate	20. "O" ring
6. "O" ring	21. Pipe plug
7. Rotating assembly	22. Cap screw
8. Piston and shoe retainer assy.	23. Pipe flange
9. Retainer plate	24. "O" ring
10. Piston and shoe assy.	25. Cap screw
11. Ball	26. Motor body
12. Spring socket	27. "O" ring
13. Compression spring	28. Port Plate
14. Spring retainer	29. Dowel pin
15. Dowel pin	30. Cap screw

31. Pipe flange
32. "O" ring
33. Port block
34. Key
35. Seal assembly
36. Cap screw
37. Seal retainer
38. "O" ring
39. Rotary seal
40. Shaft and bearing assy.
41. Lock nut
42. Lock washer
43. Ball bearings
44. Spacers
45. Shaft

Fig. 66. Exploded view of an axial piston constant displacement, fixed stroke fluid motor. (Denison Division)

probably be some air trapped in the system; this is accompanied by an erratic knock. The unit should be operated at a low pressure, up to 500 psi, and the hydraulic system should be vented until the knock disappears. At this point the pressure setting of the system relief valves may be increased to 3000 psi.

Normal Starting

The system should always be started with the pressure controls at minimum pressure. Start the prime mover and allow it to reach full speed. The pressure may now be increased gradually to the desired setting.

Low-temperature Starting Procedure

When temperature conditions are lower than operating temperature ranges recommended under Oil Specifications, the following procedure is recommended. Set the pressure controls for minimum pressure. Start the prime mover and allow the motor to reach full operating speed. The pressure controls must be slowly increased until the system temperature reaches the recommended temperature range; at this point normal operation may be resumed.

Stopping Procedure

Before the unit is stopped, reduce motor pressure to minimum and then turn off power.

Maintenance

General

Maintenance is limited to operations which do not require complete system or motor teardown; for example, repair of system or motor leaks or sticky valves. The first operation in the repair of any leak is to tighten the screws or fittings around the leakage area. If this does not remedy the leak, it may be necessary to open the motor and replace a gasket or "O" ring.

If the motor does not operate properly or there is evidence of damage, overhaul the equipment. Always refill the motor housing with clean oil upon completion of the repair operation. Use oil in accordance with the manufacturer's recommendations.

Before reassembling any parts, they must be absolutely clean and free from dirt, lint or other foreign matter. All parts must be washed in a cleaning fluid such as Stoddard solvent or equivalent. All "O" rings and gaskets must be cleaned and carefully examined for cuts or other damage. Replace any damaged parts.

The following lists possible troubles and remedies for the complete pump assembly. Perform only those operations possible under maintenance. Refer to section on overhaul procedures.

TROUBLESHOOTING

Difficulty	Possible Cause	Remedy
	Clogged filters, restriction in suction lines.	Flush filters and replace elements, remove and blow out lines.
	Air in suction lines due to loose unions.	Tighten all unions in suction lines.
Insufficient Flow	Broken shaft or coupling failure.	Replace broken parts.
	Break in piping.	Repair or replace.
	Air trapped in pressure line.	Bleed air out of pressure line.
Breakage of Rotor, Piston, Shoes, Shaft and Port Plate in Motor	Excessive pressure above motor rating.	Replace defective parts.
	Seizure due to lack of oil supply.	Replace defective part.
	Solid matter being wedged between the working parts.	Replace defective part.
Excessive Wear on the Port Plate, Shoes, Pistons and All Moving Parts.	Lack of oil supply	Replace defective part.
	Fluid medium of too low a viscosity.	Replace defective part.
	Abrasive matter in the oil being circulated through the motor.	Replace defective part.
	Sustained high pressure above maximum rating.	Replace defective part.
	Coupling misalignment.	Replace defective part.
	High overload impact pressures.	Replace defective part.
Insufficient Pressure	Pump not delivering oil.	Check oil circulation.
Overheating of Hydraulic Fluid	Operation of machine over too long a period.	Let machine stand idle. Check cooler to be certain water is circulating.
	Insufficient replenishing oil supply.	Motor must receive oil at a positive intake pressure.
Motor Making Noise	Coupling misalignment.	Realign couplings.
	Air in system.	Check unions for tightness; vent.
Shaft Seal Leaking	The face of the seal seat and the seal face might be scratched or nicked.	Replace seal seat and seal face.
	The friction ring might be slipping with shaft.	Replace friction ring.

Figure 67 shows a section through the shaft end of the fluid motor showing details of the shaft seal.

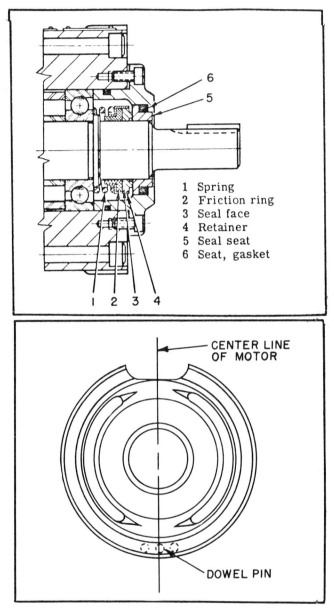

1 Spring
2 Friction ring
3 Seal face
4 Retainer
5 Seal seat
6 Seat, gasket

Fig. 67. *(Top)* Details of shaft seal of an axial piston fluid motor. Fig. 68. *(Bottom)* Diagram of port plate showing dowel pin location. (Denison Division)

Figure 68 shows a view of the port plate showing the suction and discharge ports and positioning dowel.

The following text* is included to aid the reader unfamiliar with hydraulic systems in establishing a better understanding of the disassembly and reassembly procedures and to acquaint him with instructions provided in various manufacturer's "operating and maintenance" manuals. The following applies to a 310 hp, axial piston, constant displacement, fixed stroke fluid motor.

OVERHAUL

General

The instructions contained in this section cover complete teardown of the fluid motor. Follow the order of consecutive index numbering for each illustration to disassemble the individual subassemblies. For example, Fig. 66 pertains to the motor proper. By following through from index number 1 to 45, all parts of the motor have been removed. Conversely, the components are reassembled by following the reverse order of the index numbers.

To assist in the disassembly and reassembly procedures, difficult procedures or specific operations are called out to facilitate some of the operations. Disassemble only as far as necessary to effect repair of damaged part.

Disassembly
(see Fig. 66)

Remove cap screws (1), end cap (2) and "O" ring (3). The piston and shoe retainer assembly (8) can be removed as a unit taking care not to lose the ball (11) from the hold-down assembly, and marking the position of the pistons in the cylinder barrel so that they may be reassembled in the same position. Next, remove the bearing and barrel assembly (16) by pulling on the inner bearing race. When removing this part, the port plate (28) may cling to the porting surface of the cylinder barrel due to the film of oil on the surface. The port plate is not attached to the cylinder barrel and a few light taps should cause it to break loose. The plate catches on the splined shaft (45) and can be removed later. In event that it does not catch on the spline, be careful that the port plate does not drop from the barrel after the latter has cleared the motor. In handling all parts removed, be extremely careful to keep them clean and free from harmful nicks or scratches on critical surfaces.

To remove the port plate (28) should it stick in place in the port

*From Denison Division, Abex Corporation literature.

block (33), insert on opposite sides, two brass rods of the same diameter as the width of the porting. By squeezing together on the rods, a
grip can be obtained and the plate removed. Remove cap screws (36)
and seal retainer (37). Extreme care should be taken in removing the
rotary seal (39). You can now remove the shaft and bearing assembly
by placing a brass rod inside the splined end of the shaft and tapping
lightly, the shaft and bearing assembly will fall out. Bend the ear up on
the lock washer from the shaft (45). Bearings can now be pressed off
the shaft.

Note: Mark the bearings to identify relative position. Bearings are
preloaded and must be reassembled in original position.

Cleaning. All parts must be absolutely clean and free from dirt, lint
or other foreign material. All parts of the pump must be washed with
Stoddard solvent or equivalent cleaning compound. The motor housing
must also be washed thoroughly in case of bearing failure. After all
parts are cleaned they must be protected with a light film of oil and
covered until reinstalled in the pump.

Inspection and Repair. Replace damage or substandard "O" rings,
gaskets, or seals at reassembly. Replace all worn or damaged parts. If
repair parts are not available, some moving parts may be restored and
replaced for limited service, as an emergency measure only. These parts
are the port plate, cylinder barrel, piston assembly and the cam plate.
They may be restored in the following manner:

Port Plate. Scratches that appear on the sealing bands around the
arcuate ports can be removed by hand lapping on an accurate lapping
block using an abrasive equal to Carborundum finishing compound
Grade A280V8WS. After lapping, the faces of the port plate must be
parallel within 0.001 of an inch.

Cylinder Barrel. If there has been damage or excessive wear to the
cylinder bores, there is no corrective measure possible other than re-
placement. Scratches on the face of the barrel around the cylinder ports
may be removed by hand lapping on an accurate lapping block using an
abrasive equal to Carborundum finishing compound Grade A280V8WS.
If the wear damage to the face of the barrel is excessive, a very fine
machine cut may be taken off the face, but not more than 0.010 of an
inch total should be removed and the face of the barrel must be perpen-
dicular to the spline within 0.001 of an inch. Lap face after machining
operations.

Piston Assembly. Scratches on the sealing bands of the bronze shoes
may be removed by hand lapping. To accomplish this the assembly
should be lapped as a unit with the shoe retainer as the holding fixture.
Lap on an accurate lapping block using an abrasive equal to Carborundum finishing compound Grade A280V8WS. Design clearance between

piston and cylinder barrel piston bores is from 0.0005 to 0.0010 of an inch.

Cam Plate. The working face of this piece may be lapped on an accurate lapping block using an abrasive equal to Carborundum finishing Grade A280V8WS until scratches are removed.

Caution: After lapping, all pieces should be thoroughly flushed of all lapping compound. Coat the parts with oil.

Reassembly
(*see* Fig. 66)

When assembling, the shaft and bearing assembly (40) and bearings (43) and spacers (44) must be pressed on the shaft snug against shoulder. The bearings (43) must be placed in the proper position in relation to the preload bearing condition. Direction of bearing preload is indicated on the outer race of each bearing by the word "thrust"; the thrust side of the bearings should face each other with the end of the shaft. After the bearings (43) and spacers (44) have been placed on the shaft, replace lock washer (42) and locknut (41). Inner race of first bearing must be flush against shoulder of shaft. Tighten locknut (41) and lock in place by bending an ear of lock washer (42). In placing the shaft (45) into the port block (33), insert the shaft, splined end first, through the shaft end of the port block (33). Tap the end of the shaft with a brass hammer until it fits snugly against the port block with outer race of bearing bottomed in the bore. The rotating part of the rotary seal (39) must be placed on the shaft, after shaft assembly is inserted into the port block (33). Install seal retainer (37) carefully over shaft end and compress complete seal assembly evenly and install screws (36) leaving 0.010 to 0.050 clearance between seal retainer and port block. Place "O" ring (38) on the port block pilot at the porting end of the port block. Place motor body (26), with small opening up, on a bench. Carefully insert port block (33) and shaft assembly with splined end of shaft down, into body (26). The port block (33) should be oriented with the body (26) so that the hole for dowel pin (29) will be at the bottom of the motor.

Insert the cap screws (25) into the port block (33) and secure to motor body (26). Lay the motor on its side and insert dowel pin (29). Then insert the port plate (28) through the open end of the body (26), making sure that the dowel pin holes in the port plate (28) face the porting surface of the port block (33). Figure 68 shows correct port plate installation for either clockwise or counterclockwise rotation of the shaft. The dowel pin hole must be located with dowel pin (29) as shown in Fig. 66 and also shown in Fig. 68. Be sure the port plate is not on a bind. After the port plate (28) is located, check to see that it can be moved slightly and freely by hand.

Examine all porting surfaces to be sure that they are free from burrs or scratches before replacing the cylinder barrel and bearing assembly (16) in position. In replacing the barrel assembly (16), make sure the face of the barrel is not bumped or scraped as it is installed on the splined end of the shaft and bearing assembly (40). In replacing the hold-down assembly, be sure it rests correctly in the recess of the barrel and that pin (15) is located between the barrel spline projections. Insert spring (13) in bronze spring socket (12) and place ball (11) in position in socket (12). If difficulty is encountered in holding ball (11) in position, a small amount of grease, placed in the end of socket (12) will hold the ball (11) in place.

Carefully replace piston and shoe retainer assembly (8) into the bores of the barrel assembly (16). The pistons should fit easily into the bores and should not be forced. Caution should be taken that steel ball (11) does not fall out of position as the piston assembly (8) is being installed. Attach cam plate (5) with "O" ring (6) to end cap (2) using cap screws (1). Place "O" ring (3) over pilot of end cap (2) and secure assembly to motor body (26) using cap screws (1). Make certain the high part of the cam plate (5) is located in the same position as before disassembly in order to maintain original rotation direction.

CHAPTER V

Electric Drives

Deck machinery is driven both by alternating and direct current power and a brief review of the electric motor characteristics is given here.

The DC motor in its various forms has never been surpassed for its adaptability to jobs where a wide range of torque and speed are required.

The various types of DC motors are known by the way their fields are connected to their armatures and are named, shunt, series and compound accordingly.

The shunt motor has its field shunted across its armature (in parallel with its armature). In this connection both the field and armature receive full constant voltage causing the field to generate constant flux.

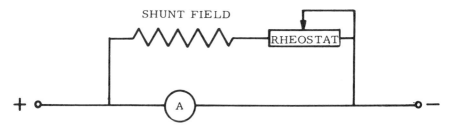

Fig. 69. Schematic diagram of a shunt wound DC motor with its field connected across its armature. The rheostat is in series with the field to provide speed control.

The changing of this flux will change the speed of the motor; so the speed control rheostat is placed in the field circuit. This varies the applied voltage to the field and in turn varies the speed. The circuit of the shunt motor is shown in Fig. 69.

The chief characteristic of a shunt motor is almost constant speed from no load to full load. This is shown in Fig. 70.

If the control rheostat was put in series with the armature, the speed would fall off as the load increased.

The series motor has its field connected in series with its armature. The same current that goes through the field goes through the armature. Because at the moment of starting the counter electromotive force

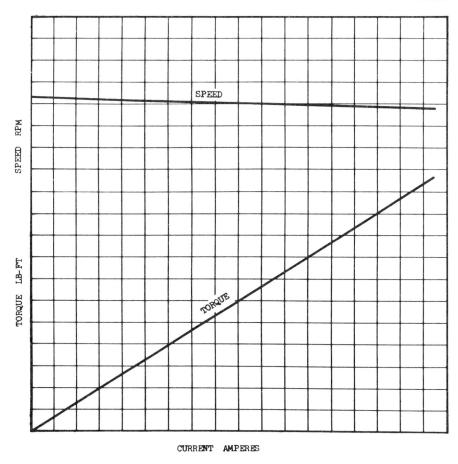

Fig. 70. Characteristic curves of the shunt wound DC motor shown in Fig. 69.

is at zero, the starting current is very high, limited only by the resistance of the field and armature. This produces an extremely high starting torque. This torque is very advantageous for slowly lifting heavy loads equal to the maximum capacity of the winch. The speed of a series motor is controlled by varying the voltage applied to the motor and this is done by inserting resistance in series with the motor and the line, as shown in Fig. 71.

SERIES FIELD

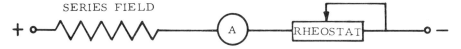

Fig. 71. Schematic diagram of a series wound DC motor with its field connected in series with its armature. The speed control rheostat is shown in series with the armature and field.

As can be seen, the motor current passes through the speed control resistors, the field and the armature. In large motors the resistors must have a high current rating to carry the full load starting current. This adds considerably to the cost of the winch control, and requires additional housing for the resistors and the heavy duty contactors and control.

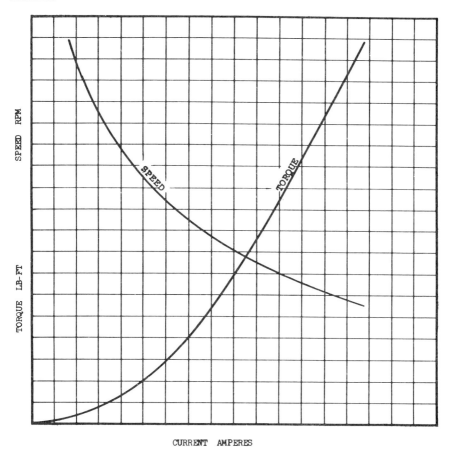

CURRENT AMPERES

Fig. 72. Characteristic curves of the series wound DC motor shown in Fig. 71.

The characteristic curves for a series motor are given in Fig. 72. It can be seen that as the torque increases the speed decreases rapidly. The torque increases to meet the load. This in turn determines the speed at a given load. An unloaded series motor will run away to a dangerously high speed and large motors will destroy themselves because of the tremendous centrifugal forces.

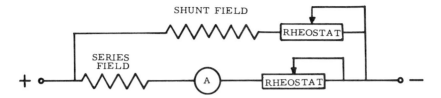

Fig. 73. Schematic diagram of a compound wound DC motor showing its series and shunt field connections and control rheostats.

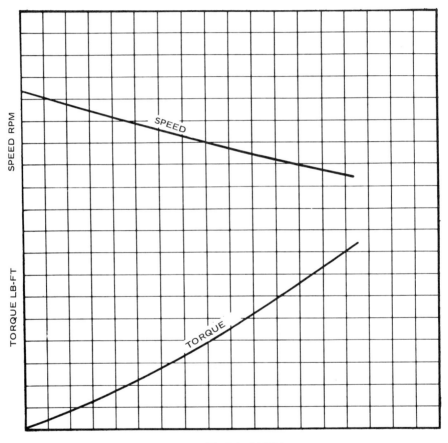

CURRENT AMPHERS

Fig. 74. Characteristic curves of the compound motor shown in Fig. 73. Note that these curves lie between those of the series motor and those of the shunt motor.

The compound motor. By combining the shunt and series connections we have a compound wound motor. This is shown schematically in Fig. 73. The characteristics of the compound lie between the shunt and series motor as shown in Fig. 74.

The DC motor can be built so that the individual field and armature connections may be brought outside the motor frame and switched externally to provide the best characteristics for the particular job. In the case of a winch, it could be switched as a series motor for hoisting because of its high torque at low speeds and switched as a shunt motor or compound for lowering.

If the motor is overhauled—that is, driven by the weight of the load—it becomes a generator. By connecting a load resistor across the motor when operating as a generator, it is forced to deliver current to this resistor. This current flowing through the armature develops an armature torque in the opposite direction; this has a retarding or braking effect on the load and is called dynamic braking or dynamic lowering. When the motor is stopped, this resistor is left connected across the motor to provide dynamic braking if the mechanical brake should fail while the load is still being hoisted or lowered. Dynamic lowering is also known as regenerative lowering. The winch motor usually has a spring held shoe or disc brake which locks the motor shaft when de-energized. These brakes are instantly released by energizing a magnet with moveable armature or solenoid operated linkage at the moment the power is applied to the winch. The brakes are capable of holding more than the rated full load of the winch.

Figure 75 is a schematic of an adjustable voltage DC winch drive. This is the type with heavy armature resistors the heavy shorting contactors which open and close under load and require considerable maintenance.

Ward-Leonard System. To overcome the objection of opening and closing heavy main line contacts and the use of heavy armature resistors, the Ward-Leonard system is used (schematically shown in Fig. 76). This system also provides excellent speed control.

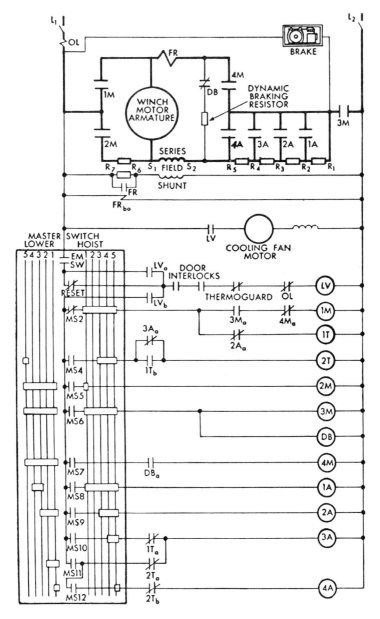

Fig. 75. Schematic diagram of an adjustable voltage DC winch
drive. (Westinghouse Electric Co.)

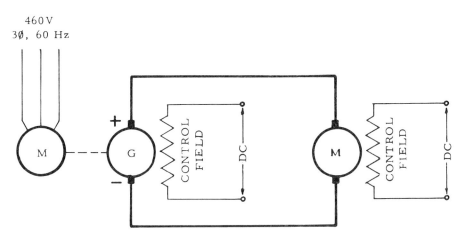

Fig. 76. Schematic diagram of the Ward-Leonard System showing the generator armature and the motor armature solidly and permanently connected in series. Reversing and speed control in either direction is accomplished by control field windings.

CARGO WINCH ELECTRIC DRIVE

The following is a description of the electrical equipment for a heavy lift cargo winch system as manufactured by the Reliance Electric Company and can be used as a general guide for similar winches.

This arrangement of equipment may be used with a Stuelcken mast for handling heavy loads or it can be used in the Burtoning operation.

The electrical system uses a modified Ward-Leonard circuit. In this system the armatures of the DC motor and the DC generator are solidly connected in a loop circuit with no switching; that is, this loop circuit is never opened. The speed control and the direction of rotation of the motor is effected by the energizing of separate fields in both the motor and the generator. The generator always turns in the same direction and is driven by a constant speed AC induction motor which operates at full voltage all the time. It is driven by the ship's 460-volt, 3-phase, 60-hertz service and is started and stopped independently of the winch equipment; that is, it is running all the time it is required to use the winches even when the winches are not operating. The control fields in both the DC generator and the DC motor require very little current and consequently the control resistors, switches, etc., are much smaller and require a minimum of maintenance.

Heavy Cargo Winch System

Electrical Specifications

*AC Motor**

Input Power .... 440-V, 3-phase, 60 hertz
Input Current ....185 amp
Horsepower Rating .... 150 hp
Speed- ....3600 rpm
Duty ....30 min.
Ambient Temperature .... 40° C.
Base Mounted

DC Generator

Output Power .... 43 KW-30 min./69 KW-
intermittent duty
Output Voltage .... 300 vdc
Output Current .... 143 amps, 30 min./230 amps,
intermittent
Speed of Rotating ....3550 rpm
Ambient Operating Temperature .... 40° C. (104° F.)
Flange Mounted

DC Winch Motor

Input Voltage .... 290 vdc
Input Current .... 144 amps
Speed (variable) .... 900/2900 rpm
Horsepower Rating .... 50 hp
Duty ....30 min.
Ambient Operating Temperature .... 40° C. (104° F.)

Note

F3-F4 excited on 180 volt, produces 2900 rpm. F1-F2, excited on 34 volts produces 900 rpm, with F3-F4 excited.

Electric Brake

Rating .... 375 lb. ft. 60 min.
intermittent duty
Coil Voltage .... 100 vdc
Coil Current ....2.3 amps
Line Voltage .... 230 vdc

*The AC drive motor has a double-ended drive shaft and flanged ends for close couple mounting of the two DC generators.

Component Description

The two boom topping winches each have a DC motor which can be clutched to drive either one of two winch drums. The main drum is used for topping and has a line pull rating of 19,600 pounds at 76 feet per minute. The auxiliary drum is used to service an auxiliary boom capable of individual operation or paired service. The line pull rating of the auxiliary drum is listed below. These ratings are based upon the line at the second layer around the drum.

Auxiliary Drum Line Pull Rating

Line Pull	Line Speed	Motor Speed
8,000 lbs. Hoist	210 fpm	900 rpm
6,250 lbs. Hoist	255 fpm	1183 rpm
5,000 lbs. Hoist	320 fpm	1394 rpm
3,000 lbs. Hoist	530 fpm	2239 rpm
1,500 lbs. Hoist	620 fpm	2641 rpm
No Load Hoist	650 fpm	2900 rpm
No Load Lower	580 fpm	2480 rpm
3,000 lbs. Lower	480 fpm	2060 rpm
5,600 lbs. Lower	380 fpm	1630 rpm

The two heavy lift cargo winches have one drum each rated at 19,600 pounds at 85 ft./min. and a gypsy head rated at 20,000 pounds at 66 ft./min.

Fig. 77. Cargo winch or mooring winch power unit. Shown are two (2) DC generators flange mounted on each end of a common AC drive motor. The motor and generator control cabinets are above, making a self-contained unit.
(Reliance Electric Co.)

Motor-Generator Set and Control. This component is comprised of two DC generators, flange mounted to an AC motor, an integrally mounted control cabinet and a circuit breaker. One motor generator set and control serves one pair of winches. This assembly is clearly shown in Fig. 77. Figure 78 shows the interior of the control cabinet.

Fig. 78. Same as Fig. 77 but with doors of control cabinets open.
(Reliance Electric Co.)

Electric Brake. Each winch motor is fitted with a magnetic brake assembly having a mechanical release. The brake is mounted on the DC motor only and not to the winch frame.

Master Switches. Shown in Figs. 79 and 80 are dual lever, self centering type. One is provided for each pair of winches. One dual switch controls the two topping winches and the other controls the two hoisting winches. Each master switch has an *ON-OFF* safety switch.

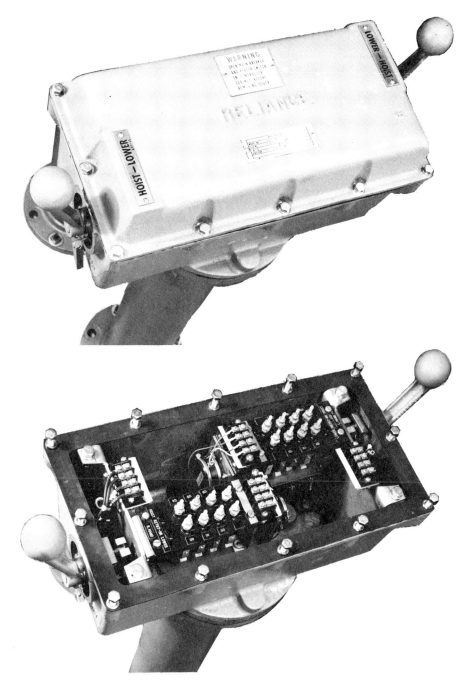

Fig. 79. *(Top)* Cargo winch master switch arranged for two (2) winches. Fig. 80. *(Bottom)* Same as Fig. 79, with cover removed. (Reliance Electric Co.)

Theory of Operation
(See Figs. 81 and 82, *in separate case.)*

The DC motor armature is connected directly to the DC generator armature with no intervening contactor or disconnect means. When not in operation, or for conditions of no control power, the normal generator field excitation sources are disconnected, and the special *suicide* field on the generator is connected to its own armature in such a way that any voltage on the generator kills itself by its own action on the suicide field.

When the master switch is in any position other than the center *OFF* position, the suicide field is disconnected and the generator main field is connected to an SCR* type voltage regulating exciter. This exciter maintains the armature voltage equal to a desired reference value which is determined by the master switch lever position.

Small movements of the master switch lever from its centered position produce small armature voltage while a full movement produces the full armature rating of 300 volts. The regulating exciter can excite either one of the generators two main fields. The fields produce opposite polarity armature voltage and, therefore, the regulator is able to produce full reversing action of the armature voltage in response to reversals in the master switch lever. The result is that the DC motor will run in the hoist or lower direction at the command of the winch operator.

Current limit function is supplied as an added feature of the reversing generator regulator. In the event that the generator armature current tends to exceed its safe commutating limit due, for instance, to excessive hook load or acceleration rates, the current limit function will automatically take over control of the regulator in preference to the operator's master switch, thus allowing the current to go no higher than the limiting value. Return to the normal manual master switch operation will occur automatically when the condition causing the overcurrent is relieved.

The speed values given for the various loads in the foregoing table are established with the master switch in its maximum position. The speed values are roughly proportional to the master switch lever positions. The different speeds for each line pull are provided for by a motor field weakening control, through the action of a motor field regulator exciter reacting to armature current.

The motor field is automatically weakened or strengthened by the regulator to the value required to produce normal full load armature current in the armature circuit, regardless of the voltage level.

The motor field excitation from the regulator is maintained at a reduced value with the master switch off and at full strength for very

---

*Silicon Controlled Rectifier.

low armature voltage to provide positive control during low speed jogging operation for hook positioning.

In the event of an AC power failure during a lift, the 1UV relay of the control drops out. This action sets the brake on the motor, removes the generator and motor field excitation and permits the generator to suicide (when the generator flux has died and the generator is producing under 70 volts). Relay 1UV is shown in Figs. 81 and 82, with its contacts in series with the shunt brake.

Closing the main circuit breaker will start the motor-generator set and apply AC power to the control transformers, 1CCT and 2CCT. Rectified DC voltage is applied immediately to motor fields F1-F2 and F3-F4. The bridge rectifier is made up of four diodes and four zener diodes; terminal 109 is positive and terminal 110 is negative.

Under voltage relay, 1UV picks up after the *ON-OFF* safety switch is closed and the master switch lever is reset to the center *OFF* position. The 1UV relay contacts supply 240 vdc control voltage to the speed reference rheostat, shunt brake, and the control. Another 1UV relay contact establishes a permissive circuit for regulator DC excitation to the generator fields.

When the master switch lever is moved in either the hoist or lower position, relay 1SR picks up to perform the following functions: a) Open generator suicide field circuit, F5-F6; b) Release brake by energizing shunt brake coil; c) Apply regulator panel output to generator field.

The master switch lever position determines the magnitude and polarity of the generator voltage by supplying the proper reference signals to the generator field section of the regulator panel. The reference signal developed by the master switch appears at terminals 159 and 165. In the hoist direction, terminal 165 is positive with respect to terminal 159. This effects a turn-on signal to the regulator, increasing the voltage output at terminals 161 and 162, which excites the hoist field of the generator. In the lower direction, terminal 159 is positive with respect to terminal 165. This effects a turn-on signal to the regulator, increasing the voltage output at terminals 161 and 163, which excites the lower field of the generator. The hoist and lower fields of the generator are differentially connected so that as the regulator provides excitation in either one or the other, the polarity of the generator armature can reverse, causing the motor to run in the appropriate direction. Generator voltage is fed back to the regulator at terminals 159 and 166, and is compared against the reference signal developed by the master switch. When the two signals are matched, satisfying the regulator, the steady state operating level is established. (The previously mentioned terminals are shown on the Motor-Generator Field Regulator Panel in Figs. 81, 82 and 83, *in separate case.*)

To limit excessive armature currents during rapid speed changes or

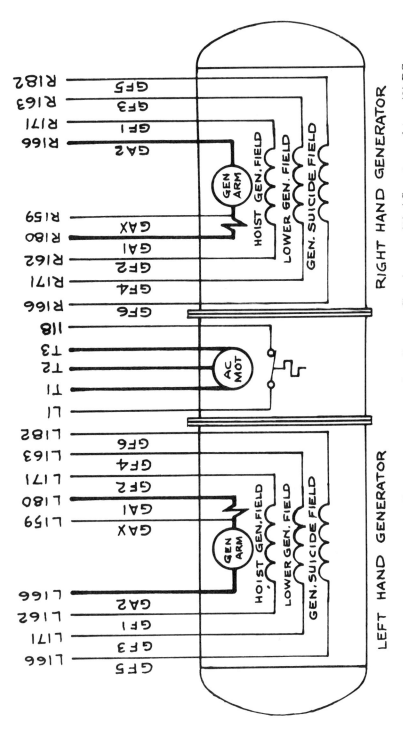

Fig. 84. Cargo Winch Motor—Generator set connection diagram. Showing one (1) AC motor and two (2) DC generators. All generator fields are shunt connected. *See* Figs. 81 and 82. (Reliance Electric Co.)

94

stalled conditions, a current limiting circuit is provided in the regulator. The voltage drop between terminals 159 and 158 is the measure of armature current which is fed back to the regulator.

Controlled excitation to the main motor field F1-F2 is also provided by the regulator. This section of the regulator senses armature voltage appearing at terminals 167 and 168, and armature current appearing at terminals 159 and 157. At low generator voltages, F1-F2 motor field excitation is at a maximum, regardless of load. As the generator voltage increases to maximum, F1-F2 motor field excitation is driven to minimum provided that excessive armature currents are not developed. Therefore, a light hook load is moved at high speeds, while heavy loads, which require greater torques, are restricted to lower speed levels. By comparing armature current against armature voltage and establishing proper excitation to motor field F1-F2, the armature current is regulated to its full load rating at all hook loads.

Field Regulator (schematic diagram Fig. 83 and wiring diagram Fig. 84). The cargo winch field regulator panel consists of two basic sections, the power section and the control section. Figure 85 is a block diagram which shows the relation of the basic components discussed in the following paragraphs.

The Power Section (*see* Fig. 83). This section converts a 60 hertz AC voltage input to three controlled variable DC outputs which are used to supply excitation to the generator hoist and lower shunt fields and to the winch motor main shunt field. This power rectification is accomplished by two full wave rectifiers for the generator fields and a half wave rectifier for the motor field. The rectifier elements, consisting of five silicon controlled rectifiers (1SCR thru 5SCR) and one silicon diode (1REC), are mounted on a common heat sink. Surge suppressing components (1SSR thru 5SSR) and bridge loading resistors (1R thru 3R) are also mounted on the same heat sink.

The silicon controlled rectifier (SCR) is a 3-junction device that conducts only in one direction and can be turned on at any point in the conducting half-cycle by means of a *gating* signal. This signal is a low voltage positive pulse applied at the gate, upsetting the *potential barrier* of the silicon junction and allowing the device to conduct. Once the SCR has been fired, the only method of stopping conduction is to reverse the applied voltage (make the anode negative and the cathode positive).* The gate lead loses control once it has *fired* the SCR. Thus, by utilizing some means of controlling the point of the half-cycle where the SCR is fired, the average DC level of the rectifier output can be varied. This control is accomplished by cardpaks which are discussed later in this section.

*If the reader is familiar with the operation of the Thyratron, the operation of the SCR may be compared to that of the Thyratron.

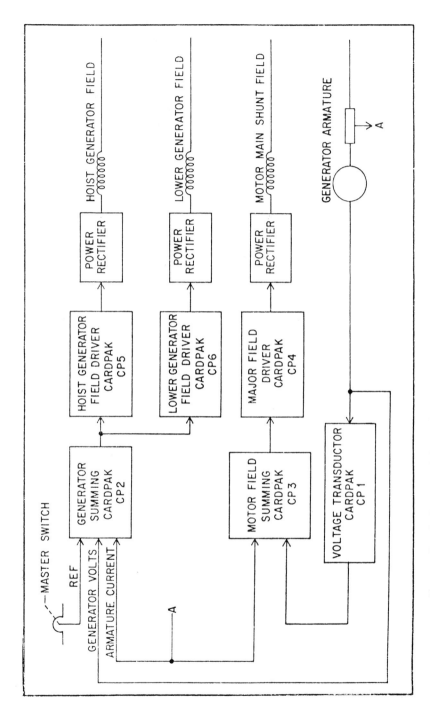

Fig. 85. Block diagram of Cargo Winch Field Regulator. (Reliance Electric Co.)

The surge suppressors (1SSR thru 5SSR) prevent the possibility of damage to the silicon-rectifier devices from the occurrence of voltage transients. The surge suppressors have a very high resistance until rated breakdown voltage is reached. Above this voltage their resistance decreases greatly and they shunt excessive peaks back through the line before they are able to reach the rectifier element.

One other component related to the power section of the regulator is an iron core step-down transformer. Its function is to scale down the incoming 440 volt line to the lower operating voltage levels for the three rectifiers, and for the 115 volt AC excitation requirement of the control section of the regulator.

The Control Section. This section of the regulator panel utilizes six plug-in modules called cardpaks. Each cardpak contains a printed circuit board which mounts and interconnects the electronic components and has all the necessary external connections brought out to terminal plugs. Each cardpak is plugged into a rack mounted on the chassis of the regulator panel and the racks are interconnected for proper regulator operation.

Three *driver* cardpaks (CP4, CP5 and CP6) are identical. Their circuits are designed to control the firing point of the SCR's.

a. CP4 controls the half-wave rectifier connected to the cargo winch motor main shunt field by operating on 5SCR.

b. CP5 controls the full wave rectifier connected to the generator hoist shunt field by operating on 1SCR and 1SCR.

c. CP6 controls the full wave rectifier connected to the generator lower shunt field by operating on 3SCR and 4SCR.

The driver cardpaks produce pulses for firing the SCR's and the point at which the pulse occurs is determined by the strength of a DC input signal to the cardpak. Cardpaks CP5 and CP6, which control the generator field rectifiers, receive their DC input signal from a common generator summing cardpak (CP2).

The Generator Summing Cardpak (CP2) is wired to the generator field driver cardpaks in a *push/pull* configuration so that the polarity of the generator summing cardpak output signal determines which of the two driver cardpaks is under control.

The three input signals to CP2 are a measure of the following control parameters:

a. A DC *reference* signal as determined by both directions of rotation and lower and hoist movements of the master switch lever. This signal appears at regulator panel terminals 165 and 159 and its level is available from zero to $\pm$ 24 volts.

b. The DC *feedback* signal from generator voltage which appears at regular panel terminals 159 and 166 and is variable from zero to $\pm$ 325 volts.

c. A DC *current limit* signal, proportional to the motor load current which appears at regulator panel terminals 158 and 159, is developed across armature circuit resistors 13R and 14R and the generator interpole and is variable from zero to $\pm$ 12 volts.

During either hoist or lower operation, the *reference* signal polarity will oppose the generator *feedback* signal polarity. These signals will establish a current equalibrium in the summing circuit components mounted on the generator summing cardpak, maintaining the required DC signal input (both polarity and magnitude) to the appropriate driver cardpak.

The current in the generator is limited to a safe commutating level and the circuitry for this is mounted in the generator summing cardpak. Should a quick movement of the master switch lever or an excessive winch load demand an extreme level of armature current, the current limit signal developed (as outlined in preceding paragraph [c]), overrides the reference signal, changing the generator output voltage in a direction to limit the armature current. The limit control utilizes a zener diode spill-over technique which is designed to clamp the driver cardpak input when the limit circuit is triggered.

The hoist generator field driver cardpak (CP5) has a bias potentiometer connected in the circuit and its function is to preset a minimum generator voltage for hoisting. The potentiometer has been factory adjusted so that when the master switch lever is moved in the hoist direction from the center position, only enough to energize relay 1SR, the generator voltage will rise to approximately 25 volts which will then develop sufficient motor torque to hold the winch load.

Note: The bias potentiometer on the lower generator field cardpak (CP6) is not connected or used.

The Motor Summing Circuit. The motor field driver cardpak (CP4) receives its DC input signal from the motor field summing cardpak (CP3). The motor field summing cardpak (CP3) receives its input signal from the following circuit parameters:

a. A DC armature current (load) signal which appears at regulator panel terminals 157 and 159. This signal is developed across armature circuit resistors 13R and 14R and the generator interpole and is variable from zero to $\pm$ 9.5 volts.

b. A DC generator voltage signal which appears at regulator panel terminals 170 and 200. This signal is developed by the voltage transductor cardpak (CP1).

The voltage transductor cardpak (CP1) is used as a signal isolating device to avoid a direct connection to the motor field summing cardpak (CP3). Its output is directly proportional to its input signal but the two are electrically isolated. The output signal, which appears at regulator panel terminals 170 and 200, has been factory adjusted so that it will vary from zero to $\pm$ 5.5 as the generator voltage is varied from zero to $\pm$ 325 volts.

The motor field is automatically weakened or strengthened by the regulator panel to a value required to produce maximum motor speed without exceeding normal full load armature current. The two signals described properly weighted in the motor field summing cardpak (CP3) produce a DC signal which is fed to the motor field driver cardpak (CP4), which in turn controls the output half-wave power rectifier bridge connected to the motor shunt field.

The motor field summing cardpak (CP3) in conjunction with the bias potentiometer mounted on the motor field driver cardpak (CP4) establishes the *standby* motor field voltage.

HEAVY LIFT CARGO WINCH
M—G SET FIELD REGULATOR PANEL

Description of Operation
(See Fig. 83, *in separate case.)*

Closing the main circuit breaker will start the M-G set and apply AC power to the control transformers 1CCT and 2CCT. Rectifier power (DC) is applied immediately to the motor fields F1-F2 and F3-F4.

Undervoltage relay 1UV is energized after the two *ON-OFF* safety switches are closed and the master switches are reset to the *OFF* position. 1UV relay contacts supply 240 volts DC control voltage to the speed reference rheostat, shunt brake and motor field section of the regulator panel. Another 1UV relay contact establishes a permissive circuit for the regulator DC excitation to the generator fields.

When the master switch is moved in either the hoist or lower direction, relay 1SR picks up to perform the following functions: 1) Opens generator suicide field circuit F5-F6; 2) Releases brake by energizing shunt brake coil; 3) Applies regulator panel output to appropriate generator field.

The master switch position determines the magnitude and polarity of the generator voltage by supplying the proper reference signal to the generator field section of the regulator panel.

The reference signal developed by the master switch appears at terminals 159 and 165 in the hoist direction. Terminal 165 is positive with reference to terminal 159. This effects a *Turn-On* signal to the regulator, increasing the voltage output at terminals 161 and 162 which excite the hoist field of the generator.

In the *lower* direction terminal 159 is positive with respect to terminal 165. This effects a *Turn-On* signal to the regulator, increasing the voltage output at terminals 161 and 163 which excite the *lower* field of the generator.

The hoist and lower fields of the generator are differentially connected so that as the regulator provides excitation to either one or the other, the polarity of the generator armature terminal GA2 will reverse causing the motor to run in the appropriate direction.

Generator voltage is fed back to the regulator at terminals 159 and 166, and is compared with the reference signal developed by the master switch. When the two signals are matched the steady state operating level is established.

To limit excessive armature currents during rapid speed changes or stalled conditions a current limiting circuit is provided in the regulator. The voltage drop between terminals 158 and 159 is a measure of the armature current which is fed back to the regulator.

Controlled excitation to the main motor field F1-F2 is also provided by the regulator. This section of the regulator senses the armature voltage appearing at terminals 167 and 168 and armature current appearing at terminals 159 and 157.

At low generator voltages, motor field F1-F2 excitation is at a maximum regardless of the load. As the generator voltage increases to maximum motor field F1-F2 excitation is driven to a minimum providing that excessive armature currents are not developed. Therefore, light hook loads are hoisted or lowered at high speeds while heavy loads which demand large armature currents are limited to lower speed levels. By comparing the armature current with the armature voltage and establishing the proper excitation of the motor shunt field F1-F2, the armature current is regulated to its full load rating at all hook loads.

Special Heavy Lift Connections. Where heavy lift winches are used a junction box is provided with sockets marked with the associated hatch number. Insert the control plug in the proper socket; that is when using Hatch No. 4 plug into socket marked *Heavy Lift Hatch No. 4* and when using Hatch No. 5 plug into socket marked *Heavy Lift Hatch No. 5*, etc.

Constant-Tension Mooring Winch Drive

The outward appearance and the control system of the mooring winch is virtually the same as the cargo winch; that is, it includes a double-ended flanged AC motor with two DC flange mounted generators complete with control cabinet and master switches.

Electrical Ratings

The electrical specifications of the AC-DC motor-generator set, the DC motors and the electric brake are listed in the following. This information is taken from Reliance Electric Company's operating manual for the constant-tension mooring winch.

Constant-Tension Mooring Winch System

Electrical Specifications

AC Motor

Input Power .... 440-V, 3-phase, 60 hz
Input Current ....73.5 amps
Rated HP .... 60 hp
Speed .... 3600 rpm
Duty ....30 min.
Ambient Temperature .... 40° C. (104° F.)
Base Mounted

DC Generator

Output Power .... 43 KW-30 min./69 KW-
intermittent duty
Output Voltage .... 300 vdc
Output Current .... 143 amps, 30 min./230 amps,
intermittent
Speed .... 3550 rpm
Ambient Operating Temperature .... 40° C. (104° F.)
Flange Mounted

DC Winch Motor

Input Voltage .... 290 vdc
Input Current .... 144 amps
Speed (variable) .... 900/2900 rpm
Rated hp .... 50 hp
Duty ....30 min.
Ambient Operating Temperature .... 40° C. (104° F.)

Electric Brake

Rating .... 375 lb. ft. 60 min.
intermittent duty
Coil Voltage .... 100 vdc
Coil Current ....2.3 amps
Line Voltage .... 230 vdc

Master Switch

Pedestal Mounted
Watertight Enclosure

It will be noted that the electrical specifications for the Mooring Winch System are the same as those of the Cargo Winches equipment with the exception that the Cargo Winch motor generator set has a 150 hp, 440-V, 3-phase AC motor as opposed to 60 hp AC motor for the Constant-Tension Mooring Winch. The Cargo winch motors may be both hoisting full load at the same time; but as a general thing only one Mooring winch will be hauling a full load at any one time.

Component Description

a. *Mooring Winches.* Each winch has a DC motor drive with an integrally mounted brake. The winch is rated at 20,000 pounds line pull at 75 ft./min. Light line speed is 200 ft./min.

b. *Master Switches.* Two sets of dual control master switches are provided for each pair of winches. These are fixed location, pedestal mounted switches. Either switch may be used to operate either winch, provided one is in the *OFF* position. However, they are interlocked in such a manner that winch operation will stop if both switches are operated simultaneously. Both switches must then be returned to the *OFF* position before resuming operation. Each switch has seven positions which are described in theory of operation (*see* Figs. 86 and 87). These master switches are usually set up at the ships rail, port and starboard sides abreast of the winches.

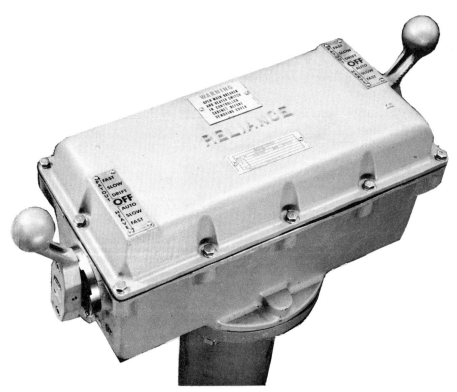

Fig. 86. Master Switch—Constant-Tension Mooring Winch. (Reliance Electric Co.)

c. *Electric Brakes.* Each winch motor is fitted with a magnetic brake assembly having a mechanical release. The brake is mounted on the DC motor only and not on the winch frame.

d. *Motor-Generator Set and Control.* This component is comprised of two DC generators flange mounted to an AC motor, and an integrally mounted control cabinet. One motor-generator set and control serves one pair of winches (*see* Figs. 77 and 78) and is physically the same as the cargo winch M.G. set and control panel.

e. *Tension Sensing Switch.* The winch is fitted with a tension sensing switch for automatic constant tension control. This will be discussed later.

Fig. 87. Master Switch—Constant-Tension Mooring Winch with cover removed.
(Reliance Electric Co.)

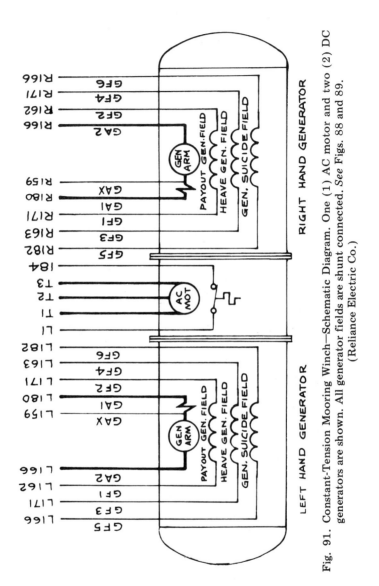

Fig. 91. Constant-Tension Mooring Winch—Schematic Diagram. One (1) AC motor and two (2) DC generators are shown. All generator fields are shunt connected. *See* Figs. 88 and 89. (Reliance Electric Co.)

104

CONSTANT-TENSION MOORING WINCH THEORY
OF OPERATION
(See Figs. 88, 89, and 90, *in separate case,* and 91.)

The theory of operation is almost the same as that of the cargo winch given previously although some of the paragraphs are identical they are given here for the sake of clarity and convenience.

The DC motor armature is connected directly to the DC generator armature with no intervening contactor or disconnect means. When not in operation, or for conditions of no control power, the normal generator field excitation sources are disconnected, and the special *suicide* field on the generator is connected to its own armature in such a way that any voltage on the generator kills itself by its own action on the suicide field.

When any master switch is in any position other than the center *OFF* position, the suicide field is disconnected and the generator's main field is connected to an SCR type voltage regulating exciter. This exciter maintains the armature voltage equal to a desired reference value which is determined by the master switch lever position and/or the position of the automatic tension switch on the winch.

The regulating exciter can excite either one of the generators two main fields. The fields produce opposite polarity armature voltage and, therefore, the regulator is able to produce full reversing action of the armature voltage in response to reversals in the master switch lever. The result is that the DC motor will run in the *heave* or *payout* direction at the command of the winch operator.

Current limit function is supplied as an added feature of the reversing generator regulator. In the event that the generator armature current tends to exceed its safe commutating limit due, for instance, to excessive load or acceleration rates, the current limit function will automatically take over control of the regulator in preference to the operator's master switch, thus allowing the current to go no higher than the limiting value. Return to the normal manual master switch operation will occur automatically when the condition causing the overcurrent is relieved. This current limiting function is also active when the drive is under control of the automatic tension switch.

In the event of an AC power failure, the under voltage relay 1UV of the control drops out. This action sets the brake on the motor, removes the generator and motor field excitation and permits the generator to suicide (when the generator flux has died and the generator is producing under 70 volts).

Each master switch has seven positions in the order *Payout Fast, Payout Slow, Drift, Off, Auto, Heave Slow,* and *Heave Fast.* The master switch is equipped with springs which return the handle from either of the payout positions to the drift position or return the handle from either of the heave positions to the automatic position if the operator removes his hand from the switch.

In the *Off* position, the brake is set and the generator is under suicide control. No motion of the winch is possible.

In the *Drift* position, the brake is released, the motor armature current is regulated to near zero, and the motor field taken to minimum value. This position allows the cable to be manually pulled off the drum with little motor resistance.

In the *Payout Slow* position, the motor is held at full field and the generator is regulated in such a way as to produce 75 ft./min. rope speed at the second layer of rope in the absence of drum friction, or slower speed down to 50% speed at full rating of the winch, proportional to the drum's resistance to turning. This resistance might be due to such factors as cable fouling, icing, etc. The control allows no more than 100% maximum motor base speed torque under this condition. With the switch in the *Payout Slow* position and rope being pulled off the drum, the motor field will automatically be weakened to speed up the motor if this condition causes the armature voltage to go above its normal 325 volt maximum value.

Warning. Rope speed must never exceed 242 ft./min. at second layer of rope. Under no condition should motor speed be forced to exceed 2900 rpm.

In the *Payout Fast* position, the motor is fully field weakened and the generator regulated in such a way as to produce approximately 242 ft./min. rope speed at the second layer of rope in the absence of excessive drum friction, or slower speeds down to stall depending on, and proportional to, the drums' resistance to turning. The control allows for a maximum of 30% of the motor base speed torque at stall under this condition. (100% armature current and 33% field strength.)

In the *Auto* position, the winch drive will respond to control of the switch in the mechanical tension error measuring system located on the winch. This switch is turned in one direction a distance proportional to the *desired* tension by setting the operator's hand lever. The switch is turned in the opposite direction a distance proportional to *actual* rope tension by the motion of a spring restrained planetary gear assembly in the winch drive train. The result is that the switch position is indicative of the error between desired tension and actual tension.

If the tension error is near or at zero, the switch is in the center or off position, since operator hand lever rotation is cancelled by actual tension rotation, and no drive action takes place. In the event tension differs from the desired value, the switch is displaced to one of three positions on either side of the zero position, depending on the direction and magnitude of the error in tension. If the tension is too light, the inhaul positions of the switch call for inhaul action of the winch to tighten up the cable. If the cable tension is too great, the payout positions of the switch call for payout action of the winch. Small tension errors (4000 lbs. to 6000 lbs.) cause the switch to go only to its first step, 6000 lbs. to 8000 lbs. errors cause the second step to come into play and still larger errors (above 8000 lbs) cause the switch to go to its third and maximum speed step. The first step causes the winch to start and pull in or payout cable at approximately 75 ft./min. (all at the second layer of rope). No correction is made for errors less than 4000 lbs. During correction, the winch is capable of supplying tension up to full winch rating.

In the case of cable tensions in excess of the maximum capability of the winch drive the winch is overhauled with cable being pulled off the winch in the payout direction. If this condition exists during inhaul, the winch stalls, due to current limit action of the generator regulator, and then actually reverses to the payout direction. If this condition exists during payout operation, the winch increases payout speed. If for any reason, whether during manual or automatic operation, and during inhaul or payout conditions, the winch is overhauled to such a speed that the current limit action of the generator to exceed its maximum payout voltage, the motor field regulator automatically weakens the motor field to speed up the winch and relieve the speed situation. Winch tension is proportionally reduced during this action. The over-speed must never exceed 242 ft./min. (at second layer), or 2900 motor rpm.

In the *Heave Slow* position, the motor is held at full field and the generator regulated to produce 75 ft./min. at light tensions, dropping off in speed to approximately 50% at the full tension capability of the winch. The switch spring returns to *Auto* when released from *Heave Slow*.

In the *Heave Fast* position of the manual switch, the motor field is weakened and the generator regulated to produce 242 ft./min. at light tensions, slowing the heavier tensions until stall is reached at approximately 30% rated winch tension. The switch spring returns to *Auto* when released from *Heave Fast*.

Operation

(Two Methods of Operation are Possible)

a. Control from Fixed Master Switches. With the master switches off, and the winch tension control lever placed in a tension position, cable may be payed out using either master switch until sufficient cable is available. The cable is placed on a bit and then the master switch is moved to the *Heave* position causing the winch to pull cable until the cable is nearly fully taken up. The switch is then released to the *Auto*

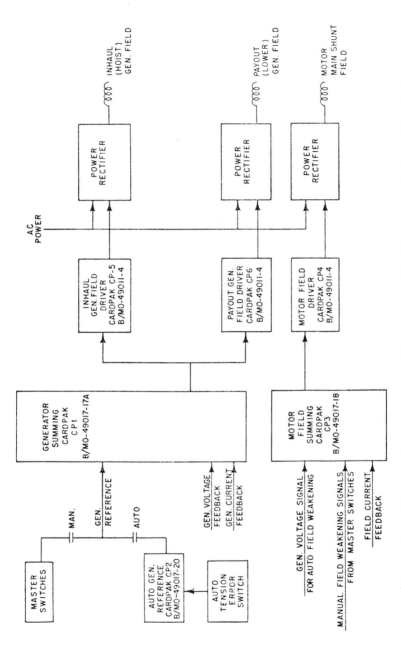

Fig. 92. Block Diagram—Constant-Tension Mooring Winch Field Regulator. (Reliance Electric Co.)

108

position to allow the winch tension error switch to control the winch until the desired tension is released.

b. Control from the Winch Tension Lever. When there is no cable tension, the winch tension switch can call for winch payout or heave in response to operator's lever motion. The winch speed then can be conveniently controlled from this position, if the fixed master is left in *Auto*. Motion of the winch tension-switch hand lever provides approximately 25, 50 and 75 ft./min. payout and heave speeds. When heaving slack cable this way, the tension control systems assume full control when cable tensions are realized.

Description of Field Regulator

The Mooring Winch Field Regulator Panel consists of two basic sections: The Power Section and the Control Section. Figure 92 is a block diagram showing the basic regulator components which are more completely described in the ensuing discussion.

Power Section (see Fig. 90). (a) The power section converts a 60 hertz AC voltage input to three controlled variable DC voltage outputs which are used to supply excitation to the generator's *haul in* and *payout* shunt fields. This power rectification is accomplished by two full wave, rectifier circuits for the generator fields, and a half wave rectifier for the motor field. The rectifier elements, consisting of five silicon-controlled rectifiers (1SCR thru 5SCR) and one silicon diode (1REC) are mounted on a common heat sink. Surge suppressing components (1SSR thru 5SSR) and loading resistors (1R thru 3R) are also mounted on the heat sink.

(b) The silicon-controlled rectifier (SCR) is a three junction device that conducts only in one direction and can be turned on at any point in the conducting half cycle by means of a *gating* signal. This signal is a low voltage positive pulse applied at the gate, upsetting the *potential barrier* of the silicon junction and allowing the device to conduct. Once the SCR has been fired, the only method of stopping conduction is to reverse the applied voltage (make the anode negative and the cathode positive). The gate lead loses control once it has *Fired* the SCR. Thus, by utilizing some means of controlling the point of the half cycle where the SCR is fired, the average DC level of the rectifier output can be varied. This controlling means will be described later in the discussion.

(c) The surge suppressors (1SSR thru 5SSR) prevent the possibility of damage to the silicon rectifier devices from the occurrence of voltage transients. The surge suppressors have a very high resistance until rated breakdown voltage is reached. Above this voltage their resistance decreases greatly and they shunt excessive peaks back through the line before they are able to reach the rectifier.

(d) One other component associated with the power section of the regulator is an iron core step-down transformer. It allows the incoming 440 volt line to be suitably stepped down to lower level operating voltages for the three rectifiers.

The transformer secondary is wound in four sections, three for the rectifiers and one for the 115 volt AC excitation requirement of the control section of the regulator.

Control Section. (a) The control section of the regulator panel utilizes six plug-in modules called cardpaks, described under the Cargo Winch section.

(b) The connections to the cardpak racks utilize a wire-wrapping technique which insures good electrical and mechanical characteristics. These wire connections are permanent and need not be disturbed when a cardpak is removed. It is only necessary to loosen two mounting screws, which lock the cardpak to its rack, and unplug the card.

Warning: Never remove or insert cardpaks without first removing power from the regulator panel by opening the circuit breaker (CB).

(c) Three of the six cardpaks are identical. These three, CP4, CP5, CP6 are classified as *driver* cardpaks and their circuits are designed to control the firing point of the SCR's. CP4 controls the half-wave rectifier connected to the constant tension mooring winch motor main shunt field by operating on 5SCR.

(d) Driver cardpak CP5 controls the full wave rectifier connected to the *inhaul* generator shunt field by operating on 1SCR and 2SCR.

(e) Driver cardpak CP6 controls the full wave rectifier connected to the *payout* generator shunt field by operating on 3SCR and 4SCR.

(f) The driver cardpaks produce pulses for firing the SCR's. The point at which the pulses occur is determined by the magnitude of a DC input signal to the cardpak.

(g) Driver cardpaks CP5 and CP6 which control the generator field rectifiers as described in preceding paragraphs, receive their DC input signal from a common *generator summing* cardpak CP1.

This cardpak is wired to the generator field driver cardpaks in a *push/pull* configuration so that the polarity of the *generator summing* cardpak output signal determines which of the two driver cards are under control.

(h) The three input signals to the *generator summing* cardpak CP1 are a measure of the following control parameters:

1. A DC *reference* signal as determined by the master switch or the auto tension error switch. This signal appears at regulator panel terminals 165-159 and its level is variable from 0 to $\pm$ 24 volts.

2. A DC *feedback* signal from generator voltage which appears at regular panel terminals 159-166 and is variable from 0 to $\pm$ 325 volts.

3. A DC *current limit* signal proportional to motor load current. This signal appearing at regulator panel terminals 158-159 developed across armature circuit resistors 13R and 14R and the generator interpole and is variable from 0 to $\pm$ 12 volts.

During either *in-haul* operation or *payout* operation the *reference* signal polarity will oppose the generator *feedback* signal polarity and at any particular operating speed (master switch at some fixed position) these signals will establish a current equilibrium in the summing circuit components mounted on the *generator summing* cardpak maintaining the required DC signal input (both polarity and magnitude) to the appropriate driver cardpak.

(i) On the *generator summing* cardpak is mounted a *gen. max. volts* potentiometer. This potentiometer has been factory adjusted and should only need readjusting if the *generator summing* cardpak is replaced. To reset, turn master switch to inhaul slow position and adjust potentiometer for 325 volts on generator armature. This should be done with winch unloaded.

(j) The generator is current limited to a safe commutating level and the circuitry for this is mounted in the *generator summing* cardpak. Should a fast movement of the master switch or the auto switch, or an excessive winch load demand extreme levels of armature current, the signal developed as outlined in h(3) overrides the reference signal, changing the generator output voltage in the direction to limit armature current. The limit control utilizes a zener diode spill-over technique which is designed to clamp the driver cardpak input when the limit circuit is triggered. The limit point has been preset at the factory, but can be reset by adjusting the slider on armature circuit resistor 13R. Moving the slider toward terminal 183 will raise the effective limit signal which then lowers the maximum armature current. If the slider is moved all the way to the 183 end of 13R, an average of 120% current limit will be established.

(k) The direction and speed at which the winch runs in response to contact closures of the automatic tension error switch on the winch is determined by the *Auto generator reference* cardpak, CP2. The auto tension switch picks up relays on CP2 in the following order and result.

Tension Error at Switch	Relays Energized	Motor Speed
None	None	0
Payout low	P	−300
Heave low	H	+300
Payout medium	P + M	−600
Heave medium	H + M	+600
Payout high	P + M + F	−900
Heave high	H + M + F	+900

CONSTANT-TENSION MOORING WINCH
M-G SET FIELD REGULATOR PANEL

Description of Operation
(See Fig. 90, *in separate case.)*

Closing the main circuit breaker will start the M-G set and apply AC power to the control transformers 1CCT and 2CCT.

Rectified power is applied immediately to the motor fields F1-F2 and F3-F4.

Undervoltage relay 1UV is energized after the two *ON-OFF* safety switches are closed and the master switches are reset to the *OFF* position.

1UV Relay contacts supply 240 volts DC control voltage to the speed reference voltage divider circuit and the shunt brake. Another 1UV relay contact establishes a permissive circuit for regulated DC excitation to the generator fields.

When a master switch is moved in either the payout or heave direction, except in the drift position of the switch, relay 1SR is energized to perform the following functions: 1) Opens generator suicide field circuit, F5-F6; 2) Releases the brake by energizing the shunt brake coil; 3) Applies regulator panel output to the appropriate generator field. Low and Medium motor speeds may be adjusted over a wide range to speeds other than the table preceding if operation requires other speeds.

(l) The *bias* potentiometer on the *generator field* driver cardpaks CP5 and CP6, Fig. 90, is set to the threshold per notes 4, 5, and 6 on the wiring diagram, Fig. 90.

(m) The *motor field driver* cardpak (CP4) receives its DC input signal from the *motor field* summing cardpak (CP3).

(n) The *motor field summing* cardpak receives input signal from the following circuit parameters, in addition to motor field current feedback:

1) Full field or weak field commands from the manual master switch position control relay MFR on the cardpak, MFR de-energized produces full field. MFR energized produces weak field.

2) An automatic field weaking circuit is used which weakens the motor field for any condition of forced overspeed requiring excessive generator voltage. Generator voltage is compared with a normal maximum generator voltage level reference, and any excessive voltage produces a signal that weakens the motor field.

The master switch position determines the magnitude and polarity of the generator voltage by supplying the proper reference signals to the generator field section of the regulator panel.

The reference signal selected by the master switch appears at terminals 159 and 165 for the manual mode of operation.

In the payout direction, terminal 165 is positive with respect to terminal 159. This effects a *Turn On* signal to the regulator increasing the voltage output at terminals 161 and 162 which excite the payout field of the generator.

In the heave direction, terminal 165 is negative with respect to terminal 159. This effects a *Turn On* signal to the regulator increasing the voltage output at terminals 161 and 163 which excite the heave field of the generator.

The payout and heave fields of the generator armature terminal GA2 will reverse causing the motor to run in the appropriate direction.

Generator voltage is fed back to the regulator terminals 159 and 166 and 167, and is compared against the reference signal selected by the master switch.

When the two signals are matched satisfying the regulator, the steady state operating level is established.

To limit excess armature currents during speed changes or stalled conditions, a current limiting circuit is provided in the regulator. The voltage drop between the terminals 159 and 158 is a measure of the armature current which is fed back to the regulator.

Moving the master switch to the payout or heave *Fast* position weakens the motor field so it will operate at twice the base speed and the motor accelerates under current limit.

When the master switch is moved to the *Drift* position, the motor field F1-F2 excitation is reduced to zero and only a current signal is fed into the regulator. This allows a minimum current to be regulated and with the motor field weakened, a minimum torque is developed by the motor. Therefore, cable may be pulled off the winch drum with the minimum amount of resistance.

The port and starboard master switches, although connected in parallel, may be operated only one at a time with the other master switch in the *OFF* position.

If one master switch is moved from the *OFF* position to any other position and the other master switch is also moved from the *OFF* position, relays 1UV and 1SR will be de-energized. The generator voltage will be reduced to zero by the suicide field F5-F6 and the brake will be set.

When the master switch is positioned to *auto*, the regulator reference is automatically transferred from low to medium to high depending on how far the automatic tension switch has moved.

In automatic control the motor remains at full field and the generator armature voltage is regulated. However, if a overhauling load should cause the generator voltage to increase above 325 volts, the motor field is weakened to maintain tension.

Terminal 168 is positive with respect to terminal 159 with the automatic tension switch moved in the payout direction.

Terminal 169 is negative with respect to terminal 159 with the automatic tension switch moved in the heave direction.

The operation of the regulator then, is the same as if the master switch was in one of the manual positions as far as the excitation of the generator fields and the generator polarity is concerned.

MOORING WINCH OPERATING INSTRUCTIONS

Tension Switch. There are six tension positions on the quadrant of the mooring winch tension control in addition to the *Neutral* position. The nominal setting of the first position corresponds to a line pull of 8,000 lbs. The winch will actually have a line pull variation of a $\pm$ 3,000 lbs. from the nominal value before the motor will be switched on to correct for an overtension or undertension condition, the line tension will return to the zone of $\pm$ 3,000 lbs. from the nominal setting, but will not necessarily correct to the nominal setting.

Raising the tension switch setting by one position will raise the line pull overtension and undertension correction points by approximately 2,400 lbs., therefore, the nominal value of this new setting is also raised by 2,400 lbs.

Manual Control. Normally, the winch should be operated from the master control. However, when it is desired to operate it by its hand control lever, this may be done by placing the master control in automatic heaving position (marked *Auto*). When this is done, if the hand lever at the winch is raised toward a vertical position, the winch will heave in cable. If the lever is lowered toward a horizontal position, the winch will payout cable.

Remote Control. The master switch is *OFF* in its center position. Rotating the handle in the counterclockwise direction will place the winch in the automatic mode. The next position in the counterclockwise direction is the slow heave position for slow heavy pulls, and the last position is the fast heave position for retrieving light line.

The first position in the clockwise direction is the *Drift* position which only releases the electric brake to allow a pull on the line to rotate the drum and payout cable. The next clockwise position is for slow payout of cable, and the last position is for fast payout of cable.

Releasing the handle from either slow payout or fast payout will allow the master switch to return to the *Drift* position. Release of the handle from slow or fast heave positions will allow the master switch to return to the automatic position.

It is of great importance that the operator, in addition to watching the man and line on the dock, must also observe that the line does not pile up when heaving or become fouled on the drum of the winch when *Payingout* wire.

Preparation for Docking. When preparing to use the mooring line, the clutch band must be tightened by setting up on the compressor wheel on the band. This compressor should be tightened enough to hold maximum tensions on the wire under normal conditions. No bars or other means of setting up should be used on the handwheel. Slippage of this band, under conditions of sudden shock or a mistake on the part of the operator, is desirable as a protection for the wire rope. *Do not* allow band lining to become rusted or stuck to clutch-brake wheel. Use light oil occasionally to lubricate and prevent band lining sticking to wheel if necessary.

Checking Procedure. When coming in to dock, preparatory to checking with the mooring lines, the tension controller lever on the winch should be latched at about the *third* or *fourth* notch from neutral (never beyond) on the quadrant. The winch should be run from the rail. Procedure should be as follows:

1. *Pay-out* sufficient line to permit putting the eye of the line over the bollard or mooring post.
2. *Heave-in* slack line as rapidly as possible.
3. Just before the line becomes tight, rapidly move the master control handle to the position marked *Auto Heaving*.
4. The winch will then check automatically and effectively.
5. If the vessel is moving too rapidly to be stopped by one *checking* operation, and before the line gets too low on the drum, move handle rapidly across the *OFF* position and over to the *Fast-Pay-Out* position so as to put slack into the line to permit its removal from the mooring post. The line should then be moved and reeled up as rapidly as possible in preparation for another *check*. Normally, the ship's screws are used backing down to assist bringing the vessel to a stop.

Caution: The master control level should never be placed in the *OFF* (center position) when checking, as this may result in the parting of the wire, due to the setting of the motor brake. The same applies to the *Fast Heaving* position. The master control handle should never be left in either the *Fast Heaving* or *Fast-Pay-Out* positions. These high speed positions are for light line use only. Handles should be kept free from binding so as to make the springs effective.

During checking operations the ship should not be moving faster than 250 FPM when on second layer of rope. Payout speed in excess of this value will cause overspeed of the winch motor.

Holding at Dock. Under ordinary conditions, while loading or unloading, a vessel can be held in position at the dock by latching the tension controller lever in about the third or fourth notch on the quadrants. Different conditions of weather and speed of loading or unloading require different settings, but all tension levers on spring lines should be set the same, unless an external force such as wind or current is impressed upon the ship. In this case raise the tension settings of winches holding against the force, or lower settings of winches pulling with the force, or do both if the external force is of exceptional magnitude. It is permissible to use any notch of *Holding*. When encountering sizable swells, use the lowest notch that will effectively hold the ship to the dock to prevent repeated corrections at high motor currents.

Shifting Operations. When it is necessary to shift the vessel along a dock, the winches with lines holding in the direction opposite to the desired motion should be released by placing the master control handle to *Drift Pay-out* whereupon placing the other winches in the *Auto* position will begin heaving the ship along the dock. The released lines will simply be pulled out, overhauling the winch. However, the master control lever *should not be left in this position* for more than thirty minutes at a time, as overheating of the magnetic brake coil will result.

If more heaving power is required, latch the tension controller lever on the winches up to higher tension settings. *DO NOT* try to start the vessel by holding the master control over in the *Fast Heave* position. To do this may result in damage to commutator, or burn out the motor.

To stop the ship place winches in *Drift* back to *Auto* and *Auto* winches to *Drift*. After the ship has stopped, place all winches back to the automatic position.

Manual Control at Winch. It is considered good practice to respool the wires on the mooring winch drums after they have become crossed over or piled up due to repeated mooring operations. This will reduce *cutting-in* and flattening of wires which eventually ruin them.

To do this easily, place the tension controller lever on the winch in *Neutral* position (as marked on quadrant plate) then set the corresponding master control lever in *Auto* and operate the winch manually by means of the tension controller lever.

This method will give slow heaving and payout speeds which are desirable when respooling. Wires should be brought out through their chocks and thence to a pair of bollards for snubbing action.

Note. It is important that the underlying layers of cable be spooled tightly and evenly and care should be exercised to insure that the wires do not become fouled again by paying out wire faster than it can run out through the mooring chocks.

Motor Generator Set. On vessels using alternating current, motor-generator sets are provided to supply current at variable voltage for the winch motors. Control power is supplied by a static exciter in the control enclosure.

These motor-generators should be started at least 15 minutes before the winches are to be used.

Clutch-band. The large brake band and handwheel with its associated compressor parts is in reality a clutch that comprises a part of the planetary system, and must be set up tight to drive the drum. The handwheel diameter, along with pitch of thread and levers, making up the compressor, are proportioned so that a good heavy pull with two hands by the average man should set up the band sufficiently to prevent any slippage of the clutch drum. The clutch should slip only when excessive loads are applied to the mooring cable. These excessive loads are encountered by loss of power, which will set the electric brake and, if the ship is moving with the cable made fast to the pier, the clutch should slip, or the line may part.

An easy, yet effective and simple means to set up on the clutch band in order to hold under all conditions, yet slip if overloaded, is to put the mooring cable eye over a bitt, loosen the clutch band and start the motor in the heave direction. Advance the tension controller lever to the last position (6) which is the maximum strain setting of the winch. The motor will run and the clutch drum under the band will turn. Set up on the ratchet handle until the winch pulls up and stops the motor. This is the maximum the winch will pull in *Automatic.* The clutch should not slip under this condition. An extra quarter of a turn on the handwheel may be necessary, after operation is started, but the clutch band should not be set up heavy with a bar, unless it is desired to use the winch for other purposes, such as a tow line to a tug, or if lifting heavy loads. Properly set, the clutch will absorb heavy high shock loads and slip before the mooring line can part.

The band lining should be oiled occasionally to prevent sticking to the clutch drum surface. This can easily be done by using a hand oil can, loosening the clutch band, making the line fast to ship's bitts, starting up the motor and oiling the clutch band as it turns. After oiling, tighten up the handwheel, letting the drum turn and slip under the band. The excess oil will squeeze out from under the band lining, some being absorbed by the lining which prevents sticking between the band and lining. Frequency of application depends on weather and moisture conditions. Once a month should be ample, less often if the lining becomes oil saturated. The compressor handwheel threads also must be kept free of paint and dirt, to avoid false hand pressure.

Note. The band should be released to allow it to slip occasionally to insure the effective performance of this safety feature.

Do not energize the motor with the drum pawl engaged. If this must be done for any reason, make sure the clutch band is completely loosened prior to energizing motor.

Electric Brake. The solenoid electric brake operates in conjunction with the motor to hold the load when power is off. Periodic checks of

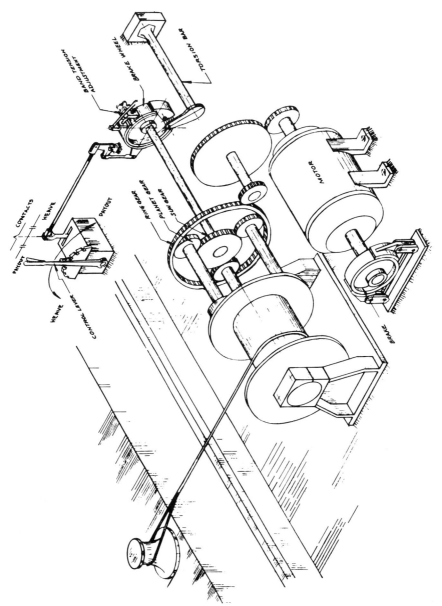

Fig. 93. Constant-Tension Mooring Winch Planetary System and Tension Control Arrangement. (Lake Shore, Inc.)

the proper lining clearance and lubrication of brake pins should be made to insure smooth and safe operation of this unit.

ELECTRIC MOORING WINCH TENSION
CONTROL INSTRUCTIONS
(*See* Figs. 93 and 94.)

Theory of Operation. To understand the principle of operation of the mooring winch, one must learn the workings of the planetary gear set. The planetary ring gear is directly geared to the motor and electric brake, and with the brake in the set position, the planetary ring gear is held fixed. The planetary pinion carrier is directly attached to the wire rope drum. The sun gear is directly attached to the drum shaft as is the clutch-brake wheel. The clutch-brake band is linked to a crank connected to the live end of the torsion rod. The opposite end of the rod is fixed to the winch base by means of an adjustable crank.

If tension is placed on the wire rope, the drum would be free to rotate if either the sun gear or the ring gear could rotate. As stated previously, the ring gear is held fixed as long as the motor brake is set. The sun gear can only rotate if the drum shaft and clutch-brake wheel rotate. If the clutch-brake band is held to the wheel; the wheel, and therefore the planet carrier, can only rotate as far as the torsion bar live end crank will let it. The more the line tension is increased at the drum, the greater is the force that is fed through the planetary gear set to the drum shaft, and hence the greater the force and movement all the way back to the torsion rod live end. The movement of the clutch-brake band is directly proportional to the tension in the wire rope when friction is discounted. This motion is fed into the tension switch through an adjustable connecting link to automatically control the winch line tension. Control and brake contactor currents are fed through the contacts on the tension switch and back to the main control panel.

The tension switch is made up of a number of sliding contact fingers which move over stationary insulated segments held in a frame. The position of these contacts is dependent upon the movement of the clutch-brake band caused by the line tension, as the line tension increases the contacts move into a new position. There are two sets of segments, one set for payout and one for heave. The automatic tension switch can be thought of as a master switch which is controlled by the line tension instead of manually controlled by the operator.

When contact fingers are located at the mid point between the two groups of segments, the electric brake is set and the motor is

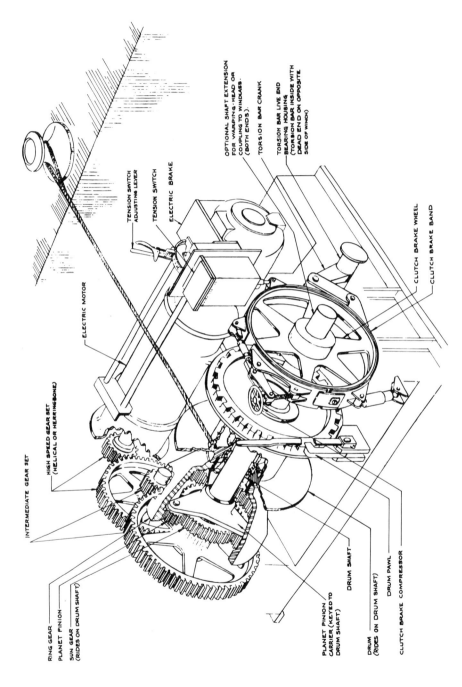

RING GEAR

PLANET PINION

SUN GEAR
(RIDES ON DRUM SHAFT)

INTERMEDIATE GEAR SET

HIGH SPEED GEAR SET
(HELICAL OR HERRINGBONE)

ELECTRIC MOTOR

TENSION SWITCH
ADJUSTING LEVER

TENSION SWITCH

ELECTRIC BRAKE

OPTIONAL SHAFT EXTENSION
FOR WARPING HEAD OR
COUPLING TO WINDLASS.
(BOTH ENDS).

TORSION BAR CRANK

TORSION BAR LIVE END

BEARING HOUSING
(TORSION BAR INSIDE WITH
DEAD END ON OPPOSITE
SIDE OF WINCH)

CLUTCH BRAKE WHEEL

CLUTCH BRAKE BAND

PLANET PINION
CARRIER (KEYED TO
DRUM SHAFT)

DRUM SHAFT

DRUM
(RIDES ON DRUM SHAFT)

DRUM PAWL

CLUTCH BRAKE COMPRESSOR

Fig. 94. Constant-Tension Mooring Winch—Detailed Assembly of Gearing and Controls. (Lake Shore, Inc.)

120

de-energized. Five speeds are provided in automatic operation, three for payout and two for heave. These speeds are dependent upon the magnitude of displacement from the mid position with the maximum speed being associated with the greatest displacement.

By raising the tension adjusting handle to one of the higher tension settings, the frame is moved so that the fingers are in contact with the heave segments. The winch then heaves in cable until the line tension matches the tension called for by the tension adjusting handle. Any further variation in line tension will make the segment board move up and down to make contact with the fingers causing proper control currents to heave or payout cable as required to maintain the desired line tension. At any position of the fingers, the clutch-brake band position can vary slightly without the segments coming into contact with the fingers to energize the motor.

To change tension setting, one need only change the adjusting handle position which locates the fingers at a new reference point.

Adjustment. Before adjustment of the tension switch is attempted, make sure that the torsion bar is properly adjusted as described in the winch manufacturer's instruction book.

Index

124

125

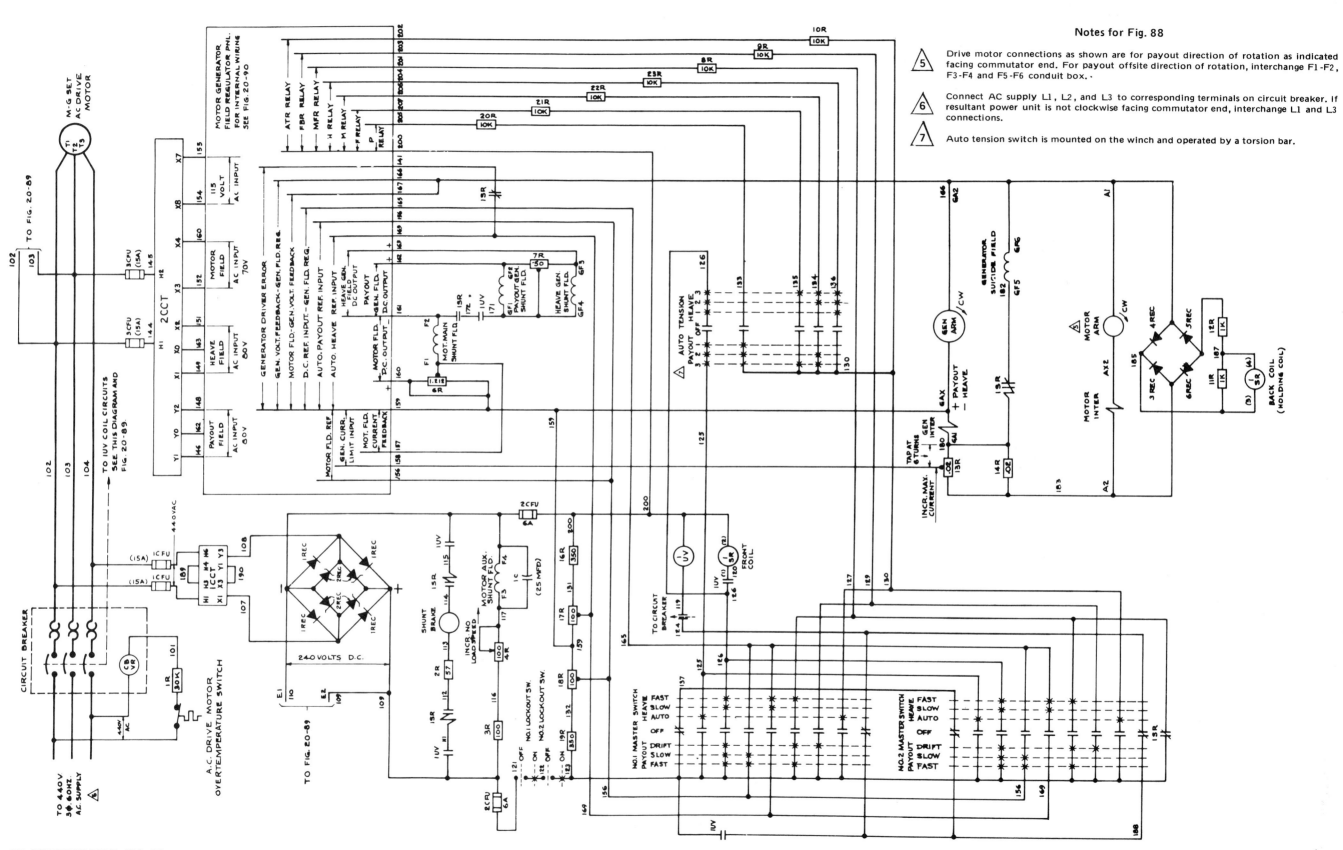

5 Drive motor connections as shown are for payout direction of rotation as indicated facing commutator end. For payout offsite direction of rotation, interchange F1-F2, F3-F4 and F5-F6 conduit box.

6 Connect AC supply L1, L2, and L3 to corresponding terminals on circuit breaker. If resultant power unit is not clockwise facing commutator end, interchange L1 and L3 connections.

7 Auto tension switch is mounted on the winch and operated by a torsion bar.

ON REVERSE SIDE, FIG. 89.

Fig. 88. Constant-Tension Mooring Winch—System Diagram. Right hand DC generator and associated DC motor. (Reliance Electric Co.)

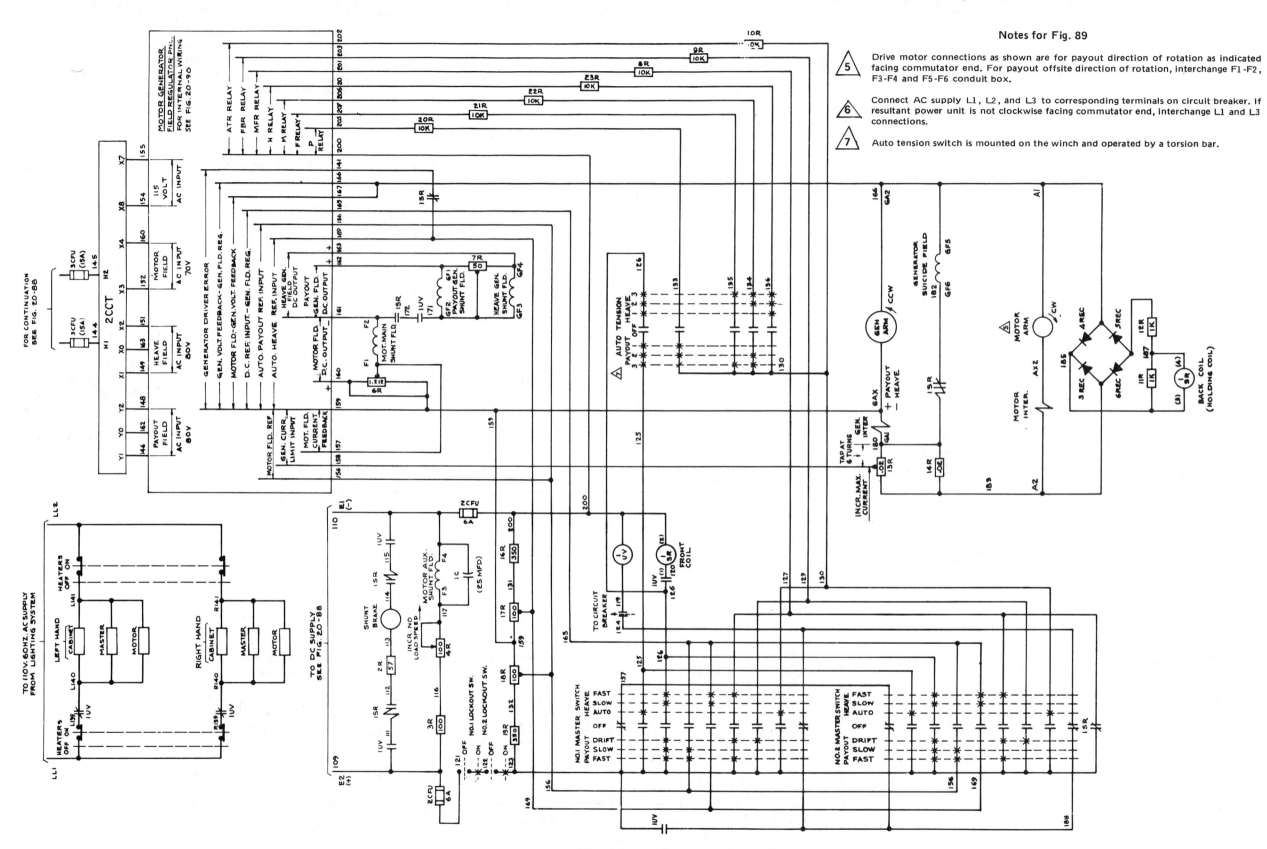

Notes for Fig. 89

Drive motor connections as shown are for payout direction of rotation as indicated facing commutator end. For payout offsite direction of rotation, interchange F1-F2, F3-F4 and F5-F6 conduit box.

Connect AC supply L1, L2, and L3 to corresponding terminals on circuit breaker. If resultant power unit is not clockwise facing commutator end, interchange L1 and L3 connections.

Auto tension switch is mounted on the winch and operated by a torsion bar.

Fig. 89. Constant-Tension Mooring Winch—System Diagram. Left hand DC generator, associated DC winch motor. (Reliance Electric Co.)

n (1)	Typ. Voltage	Type Meter
Y0	40 (4)	AC
Y0	40 (4)	AC
X0	40 (4)	AC
X0	40 (4)	AC
X4	70 (4)	AC
(2)	0	DC
	115 (4)	AC
	20 (4)	DC (3)
	0 to ± 6	DC (3)
	0	DC
	035	DC
-159	24	DC (3)
-169	24	DC (3)
	0 to ± 24 (4)	DC (3)
	0 to ± 10 (4)	DC (3)
	0 to ± 325 (4)	DC (3)
7	0 to ± 24 (4)	DC (3)
	0 to 4 (4)	DC (3)
	0 to ± 325 (4)	DC (3)

check circuit with ohmmeter.

P	M	F
	×	
	×	×
×		
×	×	
×	×	×

SYSTEM FUNCTION	RELAYS ENERGIZED			GEN. REF. 165-169	0-325 V GEN. FDBK NO LOAD 159-166
	FBR	MFR	ATR		
Payout Fast		×		+165	−166 −G42
Payout Slow				+165	−166 −GA2
Drift	×	×		0	0
Off		×		0	0
Auto		⑦	×	+0 to 24	±0 to 24
Heave Slow				−165	+168 +GA2 +166
Heave Fast		×		−165	+166 +GA2 +166

CONSTANT-TENSION MOORING WINCH
Notes for Fig. 90

Warning: Open SR coils so that motor does not run before attempting any of the following checks. Never remove or insert Cardpaks without first removing power from the panels. Do not use an ohmmeter to check semiconductors.

 Set for 320 volts no load on gen.

 Set auto. fld. weakening so that motor field starts to weaken at 360 V.

 Set completely cw.

 Set bias for 1 volt 162-161 with regulator leads 162, 163, & 141 disconnected. Recheck setting after other driver bias has been set.

 Set bias for 1 volt 163-161 with regulator lead 162, 163, & 141 disconnected. Recheck setting after other driver bias has been set.

 Factory adj.

 Mfr. energized when in auto function and 1SR de-energized.

NOTES

(1) First terminal positive with respect to second for DC voltages.
(2) Rectifier output—payout Gen. Fld.—VO to heat sink Heave Gen. Fld. XO to heat sink motor fld.—X4 to heat sink.
(3) Use DC meter with at least 5000 OHMS/volt internal resistance.
(4) If voltage is not correct, check component or line supplying this voltage.

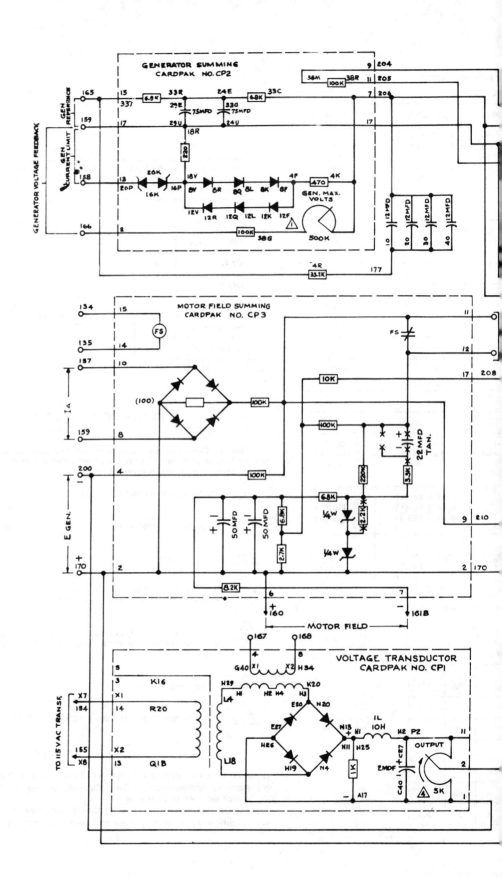

ON REVERSE SIDE, FIG. 90.

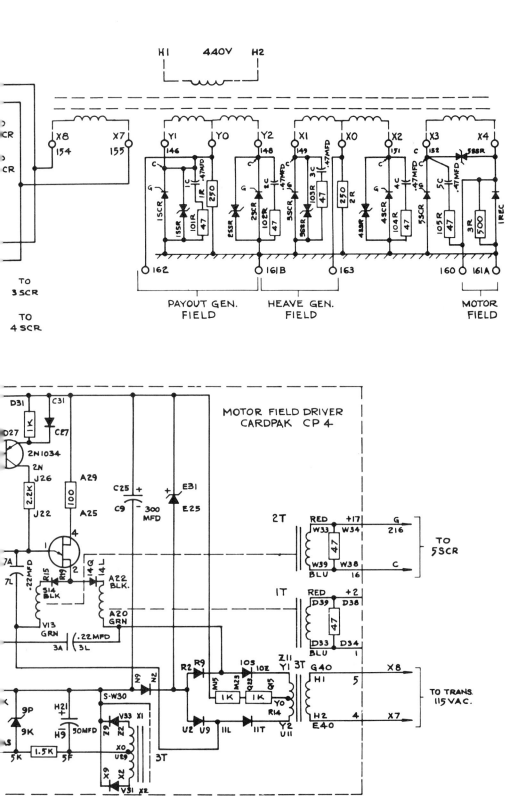

COMPONENT OPE[RATION]
Fig. [...]

Power Rectifier	Te[rminal]
AC input	Y1
	Y2
	X1
	X2
	X3
Turn power off; remove driver cards	
Turn power on	
DC output	
Turn power off. Replace driver cards	
Driver	
AC input	5–4
DC supply	7–9
DC bias-function of pot.	
Setting	8–9
Jumper Driver Pins 9 to 14 & 8 to 13	
Turn bias fully counterclockwise	
Turn bias fully clockwise	(2)
Turn power off. Remove jumpers	
Auto Generator Reference	
Reference Input	168
	159
Generator Summing	
Reference input	6–1
Limit input	8–1
Generator input	17–1
Motor Fld. Summing	
Reference input	16–
Fld. current feedback	17–
Gen. voltage feedback	17–

For further checks remove Cardpak and che[ck]
Relays may be energized with 48 VDC sourc[e]

AUT[O]

SYSTEM FUNCTION		H
Heave	Slow	X
	Med.	X
	Fast	X
Payout	Slow	
	Med.	
	Fast	

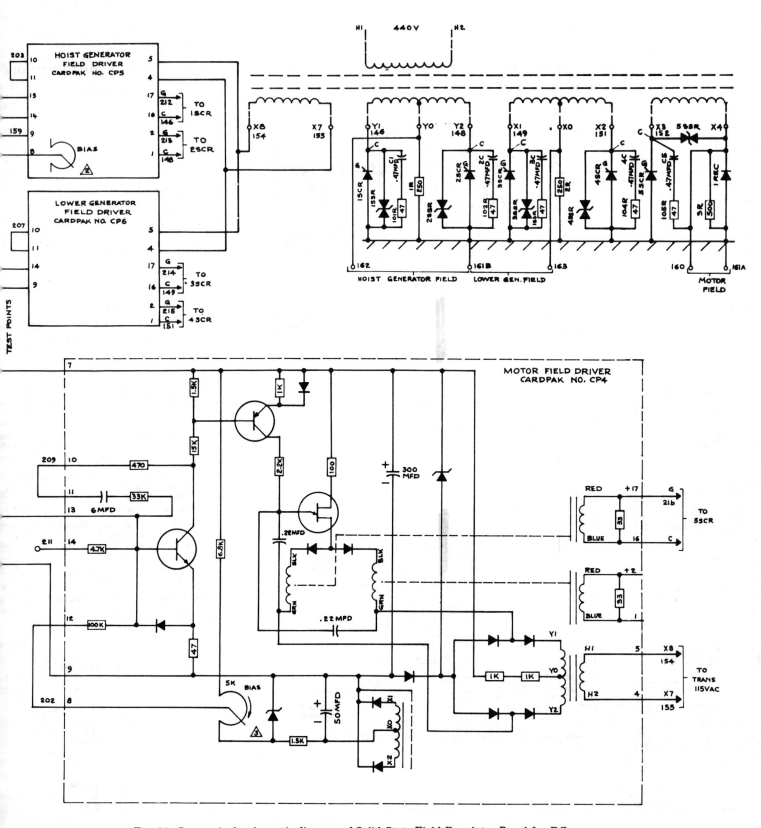

Fig. 83. Cargo winch schematic diagram of Solid State Field Regulator Panel for DC generators and associated DC motors. (Reliance Electric Co.)

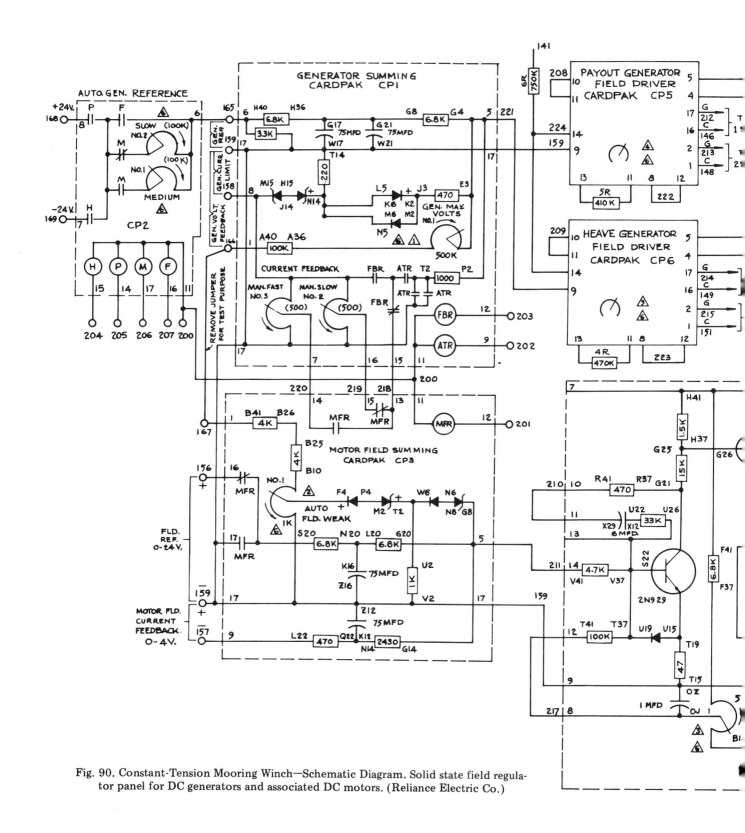

Fig. 90. Constant-Tension Mooring Winch—Schematic Diagram. Solid state field regulator panel for DC generators and associated DC motors. (Reliance Electric Co.)

Notes for Fig. 83

Power Rectifier	Term (1)		Typ. Voltage	Type Meter
AC input	Y1	Y0	40 (4)	AC
	Y2	Y0	40 (4)	AC
	X1	X0	40 (4)	AC
	X2	X0	40 (4)	AC
	X3	X4	70 (4)	AC
Turn power off. Remove driver cards. Turn power on.				
DC output	(2)		0	DC
Turn power off. Replace driver cards and remove summing cards				
Driver				
AC input	5-4		115 (4)	AC
DC supply	7-9		20	DC (3)
DC bias-function of pot setting	8-9		0 to $\pm$ 6	DC (3)
Jumper driver pins 8 to 12				
Turn bias fully counterclockwise			0	DC
Turn bias fully clockwise	(12)		35	DC
Voltage Transducer				
AC input	5-4		115 (4)	AC
DC signal input	4-8		0-3 (4)	DC (3)
DC signal output cont. Fully CW	2-1		0-15	DC (3)
Generator Summing				
Reference input	15-17		0 to $\pm$ 24 (4)	DC (3)
Limit input	13-17		0 to $\pm$ 10 (4)	DC (3)
Generator input	13-2		0 to $\pm$ 325 (4)	DC (3)
Motor field summing				
Relay input	15-14		0 or 48 (4)	DC (3)
Transductor signal	2-4		0 to 5 (4)	DC (3)
Motor field input	6-7		0 to 35 (4)	DC (3)

Further checks may be made with an ohmmeter on summing cards.

1) First terminal positive with respect to second for DC voltages.
2) Rectifier output-hoist Gen. Fld.—YO to heat sink, lower Gen. Fld.—XO to heat sink, Motor Fld.—X4 to heat sink.
3) Use DC meter with at least 5000 ohms/volt internal resistance.
4) If voltage is not correct, check component or line supplying this voltage.

COMPONENT OPERATION CHECK
Notes for Fig. 83

Warning: Open SR coil so that motor does not run before attempting any of the following checks. Never remove or insert Cardpaks without first removing power from the panels. Do not use an ohmmeter to check semiconductors.

Potentiometers as noted are factory adjusted as follows:

 Set for 320 volts no load

 Set for 25 volts minimum hoist

 Set for 13 volts motor field standby

 Set for 5.5 volts on generator

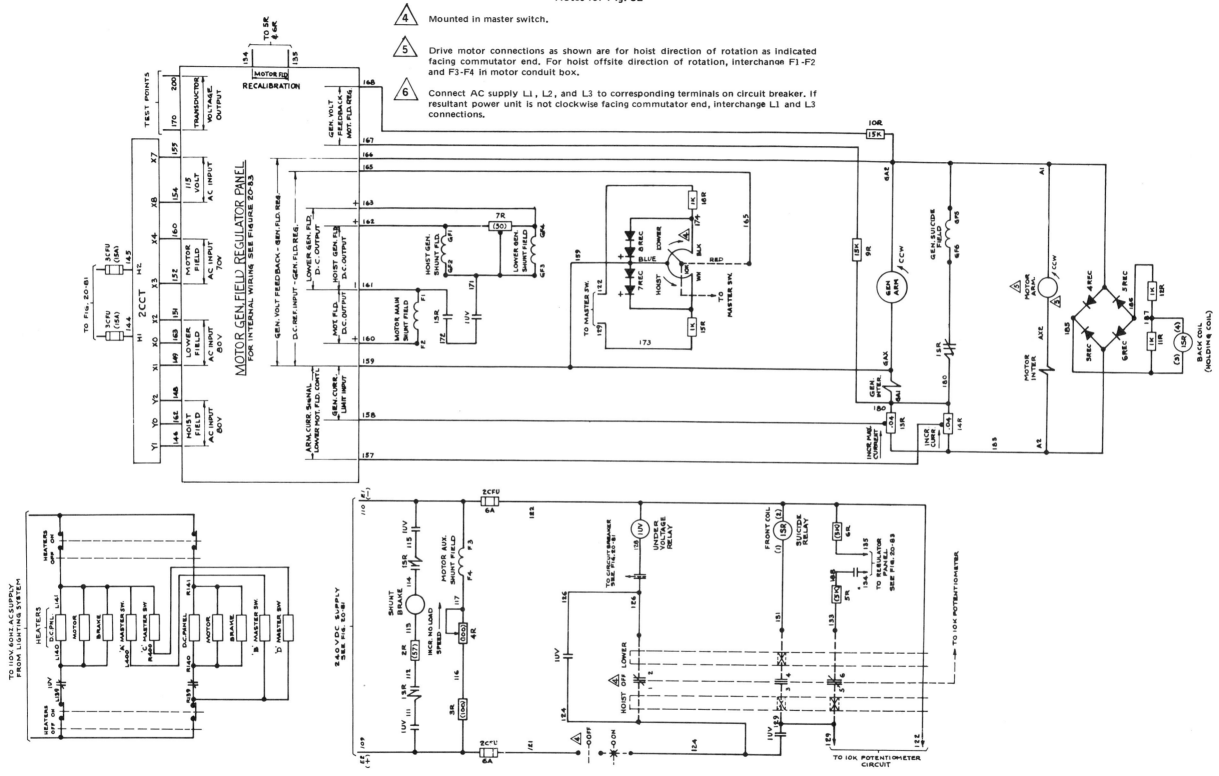

Fig. 82. Cargo winch system diagram. Left hand DC generator shown with associated DC motor and master control switch. (Reliance Electric Co.)

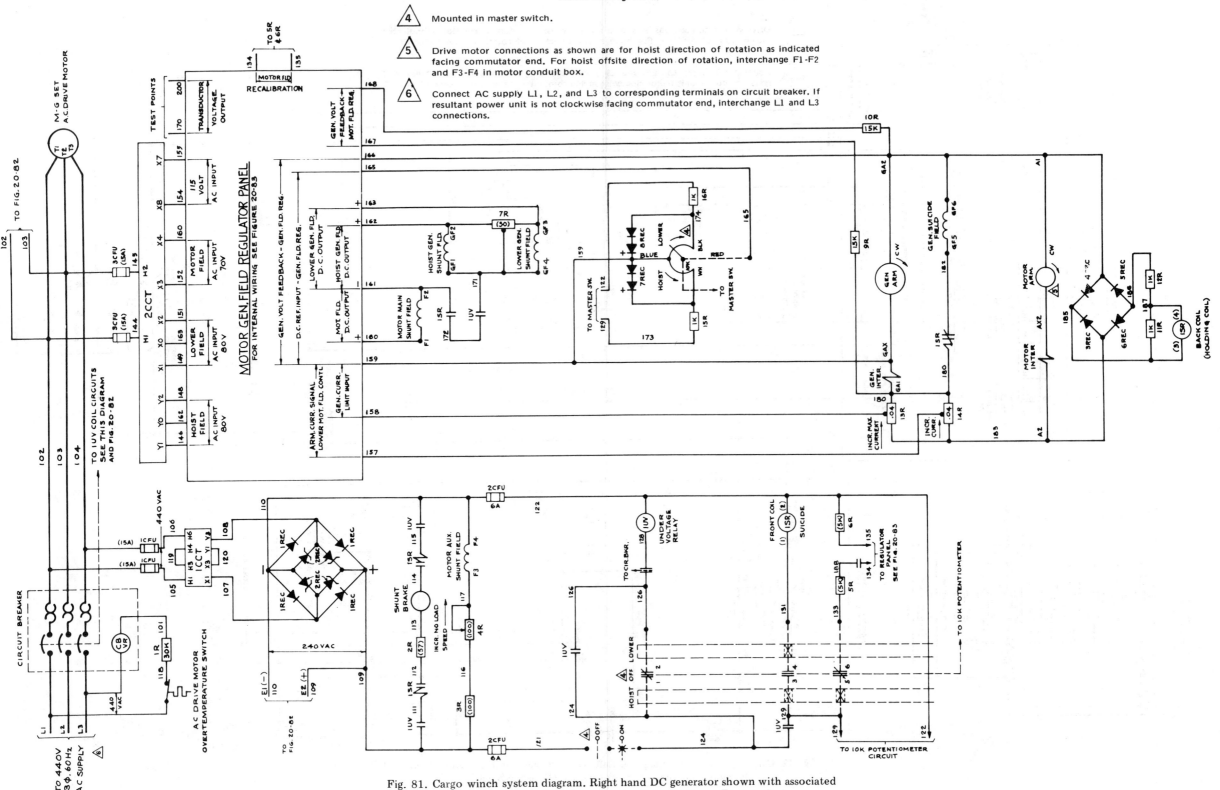

Fig. 81. Cargo winch system diagram. Right hand DC generator shown with associated DC winch motor and master control switch. (Reliance Electric Co.)

ON REVERSE SIDE, FIG. 82.